TRUCK RECOGNITION

Alan Millar

LONDON

IAN ALLAN LTD

First published 1986

ISBN 0 7110 1644 5

Published by Ian Allan Ltd, Shepperton, Surrey; and printed by Ian Allan Printing Ltd at their works at Coombelands in Runnymede, England

Below:
This 16-tonne Bedford TM1700's narrower 'D' cab is identifiable by the protruding mudguards and by the fact that the Bedford name is wider than the grille apertures behind. it.

Contents

3600 ATi
TURBO INTERCOOLING
DAF

Introduction

If you have always been confused by the identity of the 450,000-plus trucks on Britain's roads, thinking either that they may all look the same or that they must be different, but you do not know how, then this book may help make a little sense of it all.

They do not all look the same, but some are similar or even virtually identical to others, for there are many substantially common parts used on trucks built by often totally independent manufacturers. Others which seem at first glance to be identical, largely because they are built by the same manufacturer, differ in key points of detail.

Within the space available, I have attempted to describe the main types of vehicles to be found on Britain's roads, concentrating on types sold on the British market and with a cut-off period for all but the most numerous types set sometime around the mid-to-late-1960s. That allows for the life span of most trucks, from initial owner to lowly final existence, but other older types are to be found in odd corners and I apologise for their omission.

I have also taken as my definition of a truck anything over 3.5 tonnes gross vehicle weight (for an explanation of this and other 'truck-speak' see the notes in the following pages) as this is the threshold for goods vehicle testing and for the need to hold a Department of Transport operator's licence. There are some other 3.5- to 4.5-tonne vans on the market, but as these are derived from lighter vans, they are best left for another day.

Had this volume been written 10 or 20 years ago, most of the trucks in it would have been built in Britain, but this is less true today. More than one third of the new trucks being sold in Britain are built abroad, and that proportion has been growing annually. Not only that, but of the companies building in any volume in Britain, only Leyland, ERF and Dennis are British-owned. By 1985, Mercedes-Benz, the world's biggest producer of heavy trucks, had secured third place in the British truck market and was being chased by other Continental manufacturers.

Because the structure of the manufacturing industry has altered over the years, I have grouped models, where possible, under the common name by which they have most recently been built. But older makers' names are shown in text along with the heading under which details appear.

I am grateful to all who have helped me wade my way through the maze of truck types on Britain's roads and who have made their contribution towards what, I hope, is a true representation of what they may see. I am also grateful to those who have provided photographs and to *Commercial Motor* for permission to undertake this project and use its material.

If any reader has details of further points of identification of trucks, which are not covered in this volume, then please write (with photographs if possible) to the Editor, *Truck Recognition*, Ian Allan Ltd, Coombelands House, Addlestone, Weybridge, Surrey KT15 1HY.

Alan Millar
North Cheam

Front cover:
Volvo F7. All photographs were kindly supplied by the manufacturers, unless otherwise indicated.

Back cover:
Mercedes-Benz 1625. Nick Lerwill

Left:
The newest model in the Daf range is the FT3600 ATi (Advanced Turbo intercooling) 360hp tractive unit, also seen here with Space Cab finish.

What does it all mean?

Terms used to describe trucks do not all make sense if you have never encountered them before. Allow me to unravel some of the complexities.

Cabs

The cab, the area in which the driver sits on a truck, is probably the key to identifying most trucks on the road. It is upon it that the manufacturer will apply its name and other styling to tell its products apart from those of other companies. The largest companies can afford to develop cabs unique to their products, and in many cases make their own. Others share the development costs by designing them in collaboration with other manufacturers or selling cabs to others after the development work is complete. And others buy proprietary cabs from specialist firms, the most notable of which in Britain is Motor Panels.

To assist with maintenance, most cabs today are **tilt cabs**, which means that the entire assembly, complete with seats and floor, hinges forward to give access to the engine, gearbox and front axle. If it does not, then it is called a **fixed cab**. If a driver's bunk is provided, either behind his seat or above the normal roof level, then it is a **sleeper cab**. If not, it is a **day cab**.

If the cab sits behind the engine and front axle, leaving a protruding bonnet like a car's, then the truck has **normal control**. If, like the vast majority of modern trucks, the engine and front axle are under the cab, then it has **forward control**. And if the bonnet protrudes beyond the front axle, then the truck has **semi-forward control**.

Weight

The gross vehicle weight (vehicle plus load) at which a truck may operate is governed by a combination of the power of its engine and the strength and number of its axles. These regulations vary from country to country, but here we are concerned only with the British rules. The smallest trucks, from **3.5 tonnes GVW to 7.5 tonnes GVW**, bridge the gap from being large delivery vans to small lorries. They usually have smaller wheels than heavier trucks, and normally have two axles. They may be driven by holders of ordinary car driving licences and are not subject to truck speed restrictions. The next identifiable band runs to **16.3 tonnes GVW**. These usually have larger wheels than the lighter models, often spread wider apart, but with some exceptions still only have two axles. The main exceptions are brewers' lorries built with three axles to make it easier to load kegs and to spread the load more evenly. They are the first vehicles to which heavy goods vehicle driving licence and speed restrictions apply. Up to **24.4 tonnes GVW**, trucks need at least three axles, and up to **30.5 tonnes** they need four. For heavier operation, some sort of trailer must be used. Up to **32.5 tonnes** (the maximum weight before 1983), this may either be achieved by coupling a rigid lorry with two, three or four axles to a two-axle trailer to create a **drawbar combination**, or, more commonly, to couple a two-axle **tractive unit** (a truck with cab and a short section of chassis behind) to a two-axle **semi-trailer** (with both sets of wheels at the back) to create an **articulated** lorry. Some lighter articulated lorries operate with only one axle on the trailer. Up to **38 tonnes**, only articulated lorries are permitted. These may either have a two-axle tractive unit and three-axle semi-trailer (the more common form, sometimes known as the **2+3** formula) or have a three-axle tractive unit and two-axle semi-trailer (known as the **3+2** formula). Some trucks are designed for operation at up to **44 tonnes**, the weight which the EEC wants to set as a European standard, and in Britain trucks of much higher weights are used for the movement of abnormal heavy loads such as North Sea oil platforms.

Wheels

You will see references to trucks having 4×2, 6×2, 8×4 and other similar wheel layouts.

All it means is the number of wheels and the number of those which are driven by the engine and transmission. The first figure (eg the '4' in 4×2) specifies the number of wheels (ignoring twin wheels on rear axles) and the second shows how many are driven. If four wheels are driven on a six- or eight-wheel model, then the vehicle has **double-drive**, but if four are driven on a four-wheel truck it has **all-wheel-drive**. Most six-wheel tractive units are 6×2, with only one pair of wheels being driven.

Bodies

On most trucks, the bodywork starts behind or around the cab and varies greatly in design depending on the loads the truck is meant to carry. The simplest form of body is the **platform** or **flatbed** with no structure above the floor other than a bulkhead separating the cab from the load which is secured by ropes, sheets or both. **Dropside** bodies add a shallow side and back to the flatbed, and these hinge down for loading. **Tipper** bodies have fixed sides at least as deep as those on a dropside, often to the height of the cab, and unload by tipping back from rams located between the body and the chassis frame. **Box** bodies have a totally enclosed structure behind the cab. **Luton** bodies (so called because they once were built to carry light, but bulky hat boxes from Luton) have the load area extended over the cab. On heavier vehicles used to carry furniture, this is termed a **pantechnicon** (Greek for 'all art'). **Integral vans** have the cab and body built as one without any division between the two. **Curtain-sided** bodies have a solid roof and bulkhead and fabric sides and back which slide open for loading and retain the load when closed. **Tilt** bodies have fabric sides and roof which fold back for loading. Trailers have all these bodies except Luton or integral van. There are also such specialist bodies as **tankers**, **refuse collection** vehicles, **skip loaders**, **personnel carriers**, and **concrete mixers**. For heavy operation, **low loader** trailers, with the main section lower than the tractive unit, are used to ease the loading of extremely heavy equipment.

Engines

The larger manufacturers often make their own engines, diesel in almost every case, but specialist manufacturers are gaining an increasing share of business as the cost of developing more powerful and fuel efficient engines rises. Three of the engine makers have British factories. They are **Cummins** (United States-owned), **Perkins** (a subsidiary of Canadian-owned Varity Corporation) which also makes **Rolls-Royce** and **Gardner** engines . West German-based **Deutz** makes air cooled engines. Most engines now are **turbocharged**, in some cases also **charge-cooled** (sometimes called **intercooled**) to increase their power; if not, they are **naturally aspirated**. The power output is usually expressed in **horsepower (hp)**, but sometimes in the metric equivalent of **kilowatts (kW)**. If all the cylinders of the engine sit side-by-side, it is an **in-line** engine; if they fan out (to occupy less height) it is a **V- formation engine** (V6 if six-cylinder, V8 if eight).

Model numbers

There is no laid down standard for truck model numbers, but several manufacturers use a common formula by which the first two numbers indicate the maximum gross weight at which it is designed to operate and the next two or three numbers indicate either an abbreviated or full version of the horsepower rating. In some cases, the first pair of numbers on tractive units refers only to the maximum gross weight at which they could operate as rigid lorries.

Variations

Trucks are usually built in large numbers and to designs most likely to appeal to the largest number of customers, but they can be altered to suit individual needs at a later stage. Because of this, you are likely to find extra axles added later, cabs rebuilt with extra space for bunks or more staff, non-standard engines fitted later, or special features added which radically alter the appearance of the vehicle. Fire engines, to which I make only passing reference in this volume, and pantechnicons are often fitted with such special bodywork that much of the standard cab design is replaced and it may not be easy to identify the vehicle.

AEC

See Leyland

Albion

See Leyland

Atkinson

Atkinson Lorries, based at Walton-le-Dale, near Preston, was one of Britain's premier builders of long-distance haulage trucks. It remained an independent business, latterly owned 20% by Leyland, until 1970 when it was taken over by Seddon Motors. The combined Seddon Atkinson business was, in turn, acquired by the United States-owned International Harvester business in 1974.

Knight series

Country of origin: England
Weight range: 16 to 32.5 tonnes
Engines: Gardner, Cummins, Rolls-Royce, AEC
Cab/bonnet layout: Forward control

The Knight series, built between 1958 and 1968, combines contemporary and traditional design. Its wood-framed glass fibre cab with curved two-piece windscreen blends with an upright aluminium-framed exposed radiator, upon which the maker's encircled 'A' logo — similar to the graffiti of the International Anarchists — is the most distinctive feature. Most have Gardner engines, but Cummins and Rolls-Royce diesels were also fitted. Tractive units were named Silver Knight, rigid goods vehicles Black Knight, and tippers and mixers Gold Knight.

Above:
An Atkinson Black Knight with aluminium-framed radiator and shallow curved windscreen. George Brown

Above:
An Atkinson Searcher, distinguished by its deeper windscreen and glass fibre-moulded radiator. George Brown

Borderer/Defender/Leader/Searcher

Country of origin: England
Weight range: 16 to 46 tonnes
Engines: Gardner, Cummins, Rolls-Royce
Cab/bonnet layout: Forward control

The final generation of Atkinson trucks, built between 1968 and 1975, is similar in appearance to the Knight series, but has a higher cab with deeper windscreens and a dummy traditional radiator moulded in glass fibre. Borderers are four-wheel tractive units, Defenders eight-wheel rigids, Leaders six-wheel tractive units (most were rebuilt as four-wheelers), and Searchers are six-wheel rigids.

Austin

See Leyland

Bedford

Bedford Commercial Vehicles, based at Luton and Dunstable, is General Motors' (GM) principal European commercial vehicle division. Until December 1983, it was part of Vauxhall Motors, GM's British car subsidiary, but since then it has been a division of GM's Worldwide Truck and Bus Group based at Pontiac, Michigan. As such, it plays a key role in the development and manufacture of GM commercials built for use in all continents, but its main efforts are devoted to meeting British, European and Commonwealth requirements.

RL

Country of origin: England
Weight range: 8.8 tonnes
Engines: Bedford petrol or diesel
Cab/bonnet layout: Forward control

Four-wheel-drive military specification RLs, which shared a cab design with the S-type civilian Bedford of 1950, remained in production from 1952 to 1969. Most surviving examples of the 73,000 built are used by public authorities or as breakdown vehicles. The curved cab, bulging out and forward from top to bottom, suggests 1950s American styling.

Above:
A Bedford RL used for recovery work at the Erskine Bridge across the Clyde.
George Brown

Below:
A battle-weary and much butchered Bedford TJ normal control truck. George Brown

TJ

Country of origin: England
Weight range: 3.5 to 11 tonnes
Engines: Bedford petrol or diesel
Cab/bonnet layout: Normal control

The normal control TJ, first built in 1958, is still built for export markets and had clocked up 500,000 sales by 1982. Late home market examples are operated by British Telecom.

TK/KM/M

Country of origin: England
Weight range: 4 to 24 tonnes
Engines: Bedford petrol or diesel
Cab/bonnet layout: Forward control

The forward control TK was a trend setter when it was launched in September 1960, and remained in production until 1984. It was available at gross weights of up to 16 tons, mostly with diesel engines, although some customers (notably London's Fleet Street newspapers) specified petrol engines. Access to the engine is by flaps behind the cab door, beneath a short window. The quarterlights in the doors align with the windscreen, to give better visibility, but the main side windows are shallower.

The KM 16- to 24-ton model, launched six years after the TK, and badged latterly as a TK, took Bedford into a higher weight range. It shares the TK's cab, but has larger wheels and sits higher off the ground. It has wider front mudguards and a heavy double front bumper mounted above and below the headlamps and grille.

A four-wheel-drive successor to the RL, first built in 1970, is designated the M-type. It sits high off the ground, but has the TK's front bumper arrangement. It is still in production.

Above:
A Bedford TK chassis/cab being driven clear of a demountable Luton body.
Peter Rowlands

7up
WLU 850S

Left:
Beneath the disguise of its HCB-Angus coachbuilt fire engine bodywork, this is a Bedford TK. Only the grille, headlamp and bumper assembly are from the standard product.

Centre left:
A Bedford KM 16-tonner displays how the TK cab looks small on a heavier chassis. The double front bumper and twin headlamps tell it apart from its smaller cousin.
Alan Millar

Bottom left:
A four-wheel-drive Bedford M-type tanker used by the Thames Water Authority to spread organic sludges on farm land.

Below:
A Bedford TL750 box van, built for operation as a 5.7-tonne newspaper delivery van.
Peter Rowlands

TL

Country of origin: England
Weight range: 5.6 to 32.5 tonnes
Engines: Bedford petrol or diesel
Cab/bonnet layout: Forward control

Although conceived as a replacement for the TK, the TL — first built in 1980 — covers a greater weight range. It is built at gross weights from 5.6 to 32.5 tonnes in rigid and tractive unit forms. Unlike the TK, it has a tilt cab, but there is a strong family resemblance. The cab is squarer, with a heavier, but less elaborate appearance than the TK, but the stepped down quarterlights are retained.

Above:
Typical of another coachbuilding disguise of a Bedford is this Vanplan-bodied TL1500 15-tonne pantechnicon with crew facilities above the cab.

TM

Country of origin: England
Weight range: 16 to 44 tonnes
Engines: Detroit Diesel, Cummins, Bedford diesel
Cab/bonnet layout: Forward control

Just as the KM took Bedford into a new market in 1966, so the TM took it further when it was launched in 1974. It was launched as a contender for maximum-weight tractive unit business at a time when European road haulage was growing, but Bedford's success in the low-weight volume truck market has not been matched by the TM's performance. It replaced the KM range and is available as a tractive unit at gross weights between 32.5 and 44 tonnes. The tractive units were fitted initially with American-designed Detroit Diesel two-stroke engines which were noisy, thirsty and relatively unfamiliar to British customers, but now are powered by Cummins diesels; at lower weights the TM has a Bedford engine. A four-wheel-drive version has been available since 1980, and has been followed by a six-wheel-drive model. The square cab of the TM is unique to Bedford and is built in two widths, the standard 'D' cab, with prominent mudguards, and the wide 'F' cab.

Berliet

See Renault

BMC

See Leyland

Commer

See Dodge

Above:
The wider 'F' cab on a Bedford TM4400 tractive unit designed for 44-tonne operation and powered by a 14-litre Cummins engine.

Below:
A Bedford TM 4×4 with Carmichael water carrier bodywork. The large heavy-duty tyres betray its off-road capability.

Daf

Daf Trucks, based at Eindhoven in the Netherlands, has only built trucks commercially since 1950. It established a British sales subsidiary, based at Marlow, Buckinghamshire, in 1973, although its car company (since sold to Volvo) was selling trucks in Britain before that. International Harvester built up a 37% stake in the business during the 1970s, but disposed of this in 1983. Now, the company is part-owned by the van Doorne family which founded it, and by a consortium of Dutch state and business interests. It is co-operating with Spain's Enasa company in a company called Cabtech which is developing a new cab for the next generation of Dafs.

F2000/3000-Series

Country of origin: Netherlands
Weight range: 16 to 55 tonnes
Engines: Daf
Cab/bonnet layout: Forward control

The current Daf range has been built since 1970, and has a square cab design with a raked three-piece windscreen. The cab door quarterlights are slightly deeper than the main side windows. Grille designs have been modified over the years and now occupy a greater area beneath the windscreen. Model numbers, normally fixed to the grille, vary according to gross weights and engine output. The 2100, 2300 and 2500 models are powered by an 8.25-litre engine which develops between 151 and 215hp in the 2100, 215hp in the 2300, and 244hp in the 2500. They are built as both rigids and tractive units for articulated operation.

The 2800, 3300 and 3600 tractive units use an 11.6-litre engine developed from a Leyland design. It develops between 253 and 276hp in the 2800, 330hp in the 3300 and 360hp in the 3600 which was launched in 1985.

Left:
Typical of the earlier examples of the Daf F2000-series trucks is this FAD2205 8×4 tipper with a shallow, three-section grille and name badge mounted beneath the windscreen.

Below:
A Daf FT3300 38-tonne artic unit fitted with the company's Space Cab package with sleeping accommodation above the driving area and with a spoiler incorporated into the bumper area beneath the grille. The larger grille area is typical of more recent Dafs.

Dennis

Dennis Brothers, a Guildford-based bicycle and car manufacturer, built its first van in 1904 and became a highly successful manufacturer before the outbreak of World War 2. But it diminished in importance until 1973 when the Hestair Group took over and renamed it Hestair Dennis. Since then, business has been built up from a base of municipal vehicles and fire engines to re-establish the company as a low volume producer of general haulage vehicles, some export trucks and home and export market buses. In 1985, the Guildford plant — much of it built before World War 1 — was reduced to a chassis-building works; municipal vehicle building was transferred to a new Dennis Eagle factory at Warwick, truck cab building was moved to the Hestair Duple coachbuilding works at Blackpool, and fire engine bodywork was sub-contracted.

DB

Country of origin: England
Weight range: 16 to 24 tonnes
Engines: Perkins
Cab/bonnet layout: Forward control

The DB 15.5 16-tonne tipper, developed from the Pax V municipal vehicle, went into production in 1969. It has a Perkins 6.354 engine and a glass fibre cab with raked windscreen and raked-back front dash with a rectangular grille. It was followed by the DB24T Defiant 24-tonne tractive unit with turbocharged Perkins engine. Production stopped after the Hestair takeover.

Above:
Dennis developed its DB range of general haulage vehicles from its Pax V municipal truck, which used the same cab. This Pax V, operated by the Borough of Epsom and Ewell, was built as a gully emptier.

Above:
A wider grille was fitted to the glass fibre Dennis cab in the 1970s for use on fire engines and on municipal vehicles based on the Delta chassis. George Brown

Delta

Country of origin: England
Weight range: 16 tonnes
Engines: Perkins or Gardner
Cab/bonnet layout: Forward control

Dennis re-entered the truck market in 1980 with its new Delta, complete with square steel cab styled by Ogle Design. It is a 16-tonne vehicle offered either with 120hp, 154hp or 174hp Perkins engine (1612, 1616 or 1618) or with a 174hp Gardner engine (G1618). Calor Gas has been one of the regular customers for this virtually custom-built truck. Municipal Dennis vehicles have a similar cab.

Below:
Dennis's return to the truck market came with its steel-cabbed Delta 1600-Series. This refuse collection vehicle has the cab door mounted ahead of the front axle for ease of entry. Peter Rowlands

Dennison

Country of origin: Ireland
Weight range: 24 to 32.5 tonnes
Engines: Rolls-Royce, Cummins, Gardner
Cab/bonnet layout: Forward control

Dennison Truck Manufacturing, from Rathcoole near Dublin, was a short-lived Irish truck manufacturer. Like ERF, Foden and Seddon Atkinson in Britain, it used cabs, engines, axles and gearboxes from proprietary suppliers, and it enjoyed modest success from 1977 until around 1982 when the economic recession and Irish inflation squeezed it out of business.

The 6×4/8×4/4×2 models sold in Britain from 1979 for tipper and tractive unit work have square, all-steel cabs supplied by a Finnish truck builder, Sisu. The divided windscreen's corner lights make the Dennison appear similar to Daf's cabs. Most were built with Rolls-Royce engines, but Cummins and Gardner units were available.

Below:
The square lines of its Sisu cab identify a Rolls-Royce-powered Dennison 8×4 tipper.
Commercial Motor

Dodge

The Dodge name has a complex history behind it, with more changes of ownership than most manufacturers. Dodge Brothers (Britain) Ltd was an offshoot of the American Chrysler Corporation which built a range of medium-weight goods vehicles, based largely on Leyland Group components, until 1967. The origins of the greater part of the range lie with the British-owned Rootes Group, which was taken over by Chrysler in 1964 and which built Commer and Karrier goods vehicles. Commer was short for Commercial, while Karrier was a name reserved largely for the public utility market in which the company had a loyal following. All three names were used on the British market, with some overlap of ranges. In 1967, Chrysler further expanded its European empire by acquiring control of a Spanish manufacturer, Barreiros, and changed its name to Chrysler Espana. From 1976, all goods vehicles sold in Britain carried Dodge badges.

Ownership changed again in 1978 when Chrysler sold its loss-making European business to the French car manufacturer, Peugeot. Peugeot had already resold the Berliet truck business, acquired with Citroen, and in 1981 it disposed of control of Dodge to Renault Vehicules Industriels which renamed the Dunstable-based British company Karrier Motors and the Spanish company Hispavinsa. The British company has since been renamed Renault Truck Industries. The Dodge name has been kept for models on sale before the Renault takeover, although Renault badges are also carried. Ultimately, the name will be phased out as the Renault name becomes more familiar to traditional Dodge customers, especially in the public utility market where a 'British' name is still preferable.

Karrier Bantam

Country of origin: England
Weight range: 5.4 tonnes
Engines: Commer petrol or Perkins diesel
Cab/bonnet layout: Forward control

The 5-ton Bantam light truck was an early postwar (developed from pre-war) design of vehicle which remained on sale until 1973. The rounded cab originally had a two-piece windscreen, but was modernised by the fitment of a larger one-piece fixture. Petrol and diesel-engined Bantams were available, and it was a popular model for use as a dustcart, road sweeper or drain emptier.

Below:
A late-registered example of the long-running Karrier Bantam 5-tonner with its vintage cab styling and vertical grille profile.

CA cab

Country of origin: England
Weight range: 8 to 19 tonnes
Engines: Perkins, Rootes
Cab/bonnet layout: Forward control

Left:
A CA-cabbed Commer VC with box body in the United Carriers fleet.

Rootes introduced the CA cab, with its bulbous front, oblong moulding around the grille and headlamps, and slightly stepped-down quarterlights on the cab door, in 1962 and offered it on a range of 8- to 19-ton chassis designated VC. Some were also badged as Dodges from 1967. Most had Perkins diesel engines, but the Rootes TS3 two-stroke three-cylinder diesel was also available. This range was dropped in 1973.

Walk-Thru

Country of origin: England
Weight range: 4 to 5.3 tonnes
Engines: Humber petrol, Perkins diesel, electric
Cab/bonnet layout: Normal control

The 4- to 5-ton Walk-Thru, launched in 1961, was designed from the outset for parcel delivery work, as the driver could gain access to the rear of the vehicle from his cab. The two-piece windscreen and short bonnet helped give this generally square vehicle the appearance of contemporary American vans. Most have sliding cab doors, but folding side doors were fitted to some, mainly if used with a separate cab. Large numbers of Walk-Thrus, which stayed in production until 1978, were built for the Post Office. Most models sold before 1976 were badged as Commers. A few battery electric models, badged Silent Karrier, were built in the late-1970s.

Left:
A Commer Walk-Thru with sliding cab doors.

Right:
The raked cab lines distinguished the Dodge 500-Series. This one is a 24-tonne 6×4 model used to haul plant.
George Brown

500-Series

Country of origin: England
Weight range: 13 to 28 tonnes
Engines: Perkins, Cummins
Cab/bonnet layout: Forward control

The Dodge 500, available from 1965 to 1976, was a 13- to 28-ton chassis offered with Perkins and Cummins engines. Its steel tilt cab is raked sharply at the front, and the effect is reinforced by rearward sloping cab windows with quarterlights aligned with the windscreen. It has a heavy moulding around the grille and headlights.

300-Series

Country of origin: Spain
Weight range: 30 to 38 tonnes
Engines: Dodge (Barreiros)
Cab/bonnet layout: Forward control

To give it a foothold in the heavyweight tractive unit market, Dodge started to import the already ageing 275hp Barreiros 38-tonner to Britain in 1974 and offered it in tractive unit and rigid forms until imports stopped in 1982 after the Renault takeover. All British models were badged as Dodge, but it was not until 1978 that the Barreiros name was dropped in Spain. It has since been rebadged as a Renault in Spain and since 1983 has been fitted with the ex-Berliet cab from the Renault R-Series. The Spanish cab has a distinctly 1950s look, with an odd combination of curved panels and sharply cornered windows. The relatively low cab made it attractive to car transporter companies, but the 300-Series was already out of date when it was launched in Britain. It sold well as an eight-wheeled tipper.

Left:
This Walk-Thru, used for brewery deliveries, has a separate cab with folding doors, and has a larger engine compartment to accommodate a bigger engine.

Below:
A Spanish-built Dodge 300-Series tractive unit built by Barreiros. This one is coupled to a tri-axle tipping trailer for 38-tonne work.

100-Series Commando

Country of origin: England
Weight range: 7.5 to 26 tonnes
Engines: Perkins, Mercedes-Benz
Cab/bonnet layout: Forward control

Below:
Earlier Dodge Commando models have a shallow grille. This one also has the Chrysler pentstar beneath the middle 'D' in Dodge. Commercial Motor

The 7.5- to 26-tonne Commando, launched initially as a replacement for the VC in 1973 and extended up the weight range to replace the 500-Series, has a square cab with a moulding line running level with the top of the front wheels and the top of the grilles. Heavier models are identifiable by their wider front mudguards. The Commando 2, launched in 1981, is identifiable by its large rectangular grille which is in fact superimposed on the pressings for the earlier model. Most models have Perkins engines, but Mercedes-Benz engines were offered in some earlier models. The gross weight can be checked against the model number on the cab sides, starting with G08 (7.5-tonner) and running up to G26 (26-tonner).

Below:
A Karrier-badged Commando refuse collector with front-mounted exhaust system.

Bottom:
A Commando 2 G16 16-tonner with the larger grille fitted on these models. More recent ones have a Renault diamond mounted above the middle 'D' in Dodge. This one has a lorry-mounted crane with bottle bank ram fitted.

Above:
A 7.5-tonne Dodge 50-Series S75 with separate cab extended with a higher roof and extra accommodation behind the driver for roadmen.

Right:
An integral van version of the Dodge 50-Series. It only uses the bonnet assembly of the chassis/cab version, and has a much taller windscreen and doors.

50-Series

Country of origin: England
Weight range: 3.5 to 7.5 tonnes
Engines: Chrysler petrol, Perkins diesel
Cab/bonnet layout: Normal control

The 50-Series replaced and extended the scope of the Walk-Thru in 1979. It has been built in weights of between 3.5 tonnes (S35) and 6.6 tonnes (S66) and 7.5 tonnes (S75) and can either be built as an integral van like the Walk-Thru or with separate cab. In both cases, the same bonnet assembly is used. The complete cab uses pressings from an American Dodge truck design and is heavily rounded. Perkins diesel or Chrysler petrol engines are fitted, although battery electric models are also available as a factory option. Post Office 50-Series, with custom-built bodies, have two-piece windscreens.

Ebro

Motor Iberica, now controlled by Nissan, the Japanese car giant, was Ford's Spanish subsidiary until 1954. Its trucks were known as Ebro, after the Spanish river, just as Ford named its British trucks Thames until 1965. It sold a small number of left-hand drive trucks to British public utility undertakings, mostly for street sweeping work, before it made a more serious import effort in 1982. Its trucks were sold through the British Nissan organisation based at Worthing, in West Sussex.

L75

Country of origin: Spain
Weight range: 7.5 tonnes
Engines: Perkins
Cab/bonnet layout: Forward control

The first vehicle sold through the Nissan Ebro sales organisation is a 7.5-ton van fitted with a Perkins engine and a square cab with shallow side windows and plain front dash design. Few have been sold and the truck was discontinued in 1986 in favour of the smaller Trade van.

Below:
An Ebro L75 van with its characteristically small cab grafted on to a taller van body.
Commercial Motor

ERF

The story of ERF — now labelled as Britain's last independent truck manufacturer — has all the hallmarks of family intrigue, astute vision and single-minded determination that one day will make a television drama series! It was founded in 1933 when Edwin Richard Foden and his son Dennis, having lost their battle to persuade the family Foden business in Sandbach, Cheshire to forsake steam lorries for diesels, left to set up shop in the same town as a diesel-engined lorry builder. Despite even the recession of the early 1980s, which killed off plans to build a second factory at Wrexham, ERF has prospered in family control, since 1960 under the command of E. R. Foden's youngest son Peter. In 1983, it came close to agreeing a joint production deal with Hino of Japan to assemble lightweight trucks, but currency exchange rates prompted a change of policy to concentrate on developing the existing range. ERF also has a plastics subsidiary, now builds its own cabs and has a South African manufacturing subsidiary.

KV-Series

Country of origin: England
Weight range: up to 30 tonnes
Engines: Gardner
Cab/bonnet layout: Forward control

A handful of ERF KVs survive in service in Britain. This classic design, built from 1953 until 1962, has a rounded glass fibre cab built by Jennings of Sandbach (taken over by ERF in the 1960s) and fitted with curved, two-piece windscreens and an oval grille with triangular mouldings either side. Those built from 1960-62 have twin headlamps. Most have Gardner engines.

Below:
An immaculate ERF KV-Series platform truck still in service in 1985 with an Ayrshire potato merchant. The plastic ERF name is from a newer design. George Brown.

LV/A-Series

Country of origin: England
Weight range: up to 42 tonnes and heavy haulage
Engines: Gardner, Perkins, Rolls-Royce, Cummins
Cab/bonnet layout: Forward control

In place of the trend-setting KV, ERF developed its LV in 1962. It, too, has a glass fibre cab, but it is squarer in profile, with a single-piece curved windscreen. Those built before 1970 have a shallow grille and chrome fluting above and below the grille. By the late 1960s, they were fitted with a slightly deeper cab door quarterlight. From 1970, when it was renamed the A-Series, the chrome was discarded and a large rectangular grille fitted. This range was built from 16-tonner to maximum-weight artic, with engines by Gardner, Perkins, Rolls-Royce and Cummins. From 1972 to 1976, the Motor Panels steel cab — similar to that used by Guy, Scammell and Seddon — was fitted as an option. It had already been used for export and heavy haulage vehicles, and was used as the basis of the cab of the ERF European, a Cummins 14-litre engined 42-ton international haulage tractive unit launched in 1973 and built in relatively small numbers. The European had a horizontally slatted grille occupying the full width of the front dash and protruding from the area below the windscreen.

Below:
A Cummins-engined ERF LV built for refuse disposal work.

Bottom:
The larger grille identifies the ERF A-Series, seen here in Gardner-engined four-wheel form. George Brown

Right:
A Motor Panels cab on a 34-tonne ERF tractive unit powered by a Gardner 8LXB 240hp engine.

Below right:
ERF European tractive units with their distinctive large horizontally-slatted grilles and Motor Panels cabs.

B-Series

Country of origin: England
Weight range: 16 to 40 tonnes
Engines: Gardner, Cummins, Rolls-Royce
Cab/bonnet layout: Forward control

Production of the B-Series was phased in from 1974 to 1977, as first the A-Series and then the Motor Panels ERFs were dropped, and continued until 1981. Its square-styled SP cab has a steel frame panelled in sheet-moulded compound (a plastics material). The cab doors have no quarterlights, and the grille is slatted horizontally and vertically and occupies most of the front dash beneath the windscreen. It was built in versions from 16-ton to top weight artic with Gardner, Cummins and Rolls-Royce engines.

Above:
An ERF B-Series tractive unit uprated for 38-tonne work by fitting an additional lifting axle. The curtain-sided trailer shows how traditional signwriting can be applied to modern fabric.

Above right:
An ERF E10 4×2 tractive unit operated by United Transport Tankers, part of the BET group. Distinguishing features include the air intake stack above the cab, the square headlamps and grille corner flash. The badge on the nearside bumper is an exemption permit plate for the Greater London night and weekend lorry ban introduced in January 1986.

C-Series

Country of origin: England
Weight range: 16 to 40 tonnes
Engines: Gardner, Cummins, Rolls-Royce
Cab/bonnet layout: Forward control

The C-Series, which replaced the B-Series in 1981, has a lighter version of the SP cab, identifiable externally by its shallower horizontally-slatted and chrome-surrounded grille. Options are similar to those for the B-Series, but the company now concentrates production effort on the CP package with Cummins L10 and 14-litre engines

E-Series

Country of origin: England
Weight range: 16 to 40 tonnes
Engines: Cummins, Gardner, Perkins Eagle
Cab/bonnet layout: Forward control

When the C-Series was superseded in 1986, ERF skipped a letter to avoid any confusion with Ford's D-Series, but clung on to the basic SP (by now designated SP4) smc cab. The main differences are a squarer profile with new roof and squared off panelling behind the cab door, a single air intake stack behind the cab, rectangular headlamps from the M16, lower mounted front indicator lamps, and a restyled radiator grille with corner flash on the offside top. The standard tractive units, extending the CP concept from the previous range, are designated E10 if fitted with the Cummins L10 and E14 if fitted with the same manufacturer's 14-litre unit. Gardner and Perkins Eagle engines are also offered as options. Later in 1986, the E6 16.3-tonner, powered by Cummins' Darlington-built B-Series 5.9-litre engine developing 180hp, replaced the M16. It has a shorter version of the SP4 cab, without the squared-off rear.

M-Series

Country of origin: England
Weight range: 16 tonnes
Engines: Gardner, Perkins, Dorman
Cab/bonnet layout: Forward control

In an effort to sell more trucks in the volume 16-tonne market, ERF developed a lighter truck, the M-Series, which was launched in 1978 as a four-wheel 16-tonner and a six-wheel 24-tonner. It uses a lower version of the SP cab (with B-Series grille) and in its initial form was offered with either a 155hp Gardner 6LXB engine or a Dorman diesel. It sold only in small numbers and in 1983 was replaced by the M16, a lighter 16-tonner powered by a Perkins T6 354.4 or Gardner diesel and fitted with C-Series grille.

Below:
A Gardner-engined ERF M16 livestock transporter with the style of CP cab also used on the C-Series.

Fiat

See Iveco.

Foden

The Sandbach, Cheshire firm of Fodens started building steam wagons in 1901, although it had been in the steam engineering business for many years before that. It came close to collapse in 1933, when E. R. Foden resigned to set up ERF and demand for its steam vehicles evaporated before it geared itself up to producing diesel-engined trucks. However, it clawed its way back and even built its own two-stroke diesel engines from 1947 until the early 1970s. A new factory, based on lessons learned from a Scania plant in Sweden, was built in 1973, but the company nearly collapsed a year later and was rescued by City business interests. It recovered until the 1980 recession finally drove the still family-owned business into receivership and it was taken over by Paccar, the American group which also makes Kenworth and Peterbilt trucks. A new management team, American initially, moved in and developed a build-to-order policy designed to give customers a wide choice of engines, axles and gearboxes. It built Ford's Transcontinental truck for the last year of its existence, and more recently has built Kenworth trucks for customers in the Middle East. After the Paccar takeover, the business was named Sandbach Engineering pending the settlement of the old company's debts, but it is now called Foden Trucks.

S21

Country of origin: England
Weight range: up to 24 tonnes
Engines: Foden, Gardner
Cab/bonnet layout: Forward control

As with most makes, the Foden range is most easily identified by its cab, even though there may be fundamental differences at chassis level. The S21 'Sputnik' cab of 1957 is a case in point, being fitted to a range of FE (Foden-engined) and FG (Gardner-engined) trucks. Its round cab with two-piece curved windscreen and flowing lines is typical of the period.

Below:
A Foden S21-cabbed tractive unit attached to a Blue Circle cement semi-trailer.

S34/S36/S39

Country of origin: England
Weight range: up to 32.5 tonnes
Engines: Foden, Gardner, Cummins, Rolls-Royce
Cab/bonnet layout: Forward control

Foden was at the forefront of British truck technology in 1962 when it launched its S34 cab, its first tilt cab and one of the first such cabs available on a production truck, rather than from a specialist conversion company. It is larger than the S21, has a single-piece windscreen, and larger cab door windows with recessed quarterlights. It spearheaded the company's entry in 1964 into the then new market for 32.5-tonners. The S36, launched in 1966, is a non-tilt cab variant with twin headlamps rather than single square

Above:
Tilt-cab Foden S34s have single-piece windscreens and square headlamps.
Peter Rowlands

Right:
A Foden S36 fixed cab on an articulated tipping outfit. S36s were built with horizontally-angled pairs of headlamps, like this truck.

Above:
The Foden Sixer lightweight tipper/mixer of 1976 revived the compact S39 cab with its two-piece windscreen. Peter Rowlands

lamps as on the S36. The slightly taller S39, with divided windscreen to suit tipper operators worried about windscreen breakages, also appeared in 1966 and was destined to remain in production longest as it was revived in 1976 when the Gardner-engined lightweight Sixer tipper/mixer was launched. The introduction of 32.5-tonners added Cummins and Rolls-Royce engines to the range of power units available on Fodens while these glass fibred cabs were in production.

S40/S50/S60/S70

Country of origin: England
Weight range: 30 to 44 tonnes
Engines: Gardner, Cummins, Rolls-Royce
Cab/bonnet layout: Forward control

The S36 and S39 were followed by optional steel cabs for operators looking for a stronger product. The S40 was the standard Motor Panels, as fitted to ERFs, but was distinguished by a Foden grille and the V-shaped mouldings common to trucks with Foden cabs. The Sandbach-built S50 and S60 also have the characteristic grille and mouldings, but sport a short-lived and none-too-popular square design of cab with a

Below left:
The standard Motor Panels cab is partially disguised by Foden's grille styling which protrudes forward of the windscreen. This is the S40 cab, in this case on an eight-wheel scrap metal dumper.

Right:
A relatively rare Foden S50 half-cab eight-wheel tipper. The half-cab reduced the risk of cab damage on off-road work and was also fitted to some tractive units.

Below:
The S60/S70 full-width cab had the same short-lived styling of the S50.

reverse-raked windscreen arrangement. The S50 is particularly unconventional on account of its one-man half-cab, while the S60 is a full width design with two-piece windscreen. The S70 is a glass fibre version of the S60.

S80/S83

Country of origin: England
Weight range: 24 to 44 tonnes
Engines: Gardner, Cummins, Rolls-Royce
Cab/bonnet layout: Forward control

Foden's final design of glass fibre cab, the S80, appeared in 1972 after two-stroke engine production ended. Like the bizarre S50 and S60, it is square in profile, but the two-piece windscreen is raked conventionally and less severely; it has a square grille with

Above:
A Foden S80/S83-cabbed tractive unit. The design suffers from having a narrow cab door. Peter Rowlands

kite-shaped Foden moulding, and has comparatively narrow cab doors and separate quarterlights. Military versions were supplied until 1977.

S90/S95

Country of origin: England
Weight range: 24 to 44 tonnes
Engines: Gardner, Cummins, Rolls-Royce
Cab/bonnet layout: Forward control

The gradual change from building trucks from its own components, to buying in axles, gearboxes and cabs as well as engines, began with the introduction of the S90 Motor Panels steel cab in 1974, and gathered momentum as the company restructured its activities after its near-collapse to develop its 1977 S95-cab Fleetmaster high-specification tractive unit and S90-cab Haulmaster lower-specification general haulage and tipper models. The Fleetmaster has a single-piece curved windscreen and shallow grille, the Haulmaster a two-piece windscreen and deeper grille. The cab door is wider than on the S80 and incorporates quarterlights.

S10

Country of origin: England
Weight range: 24 to 44 tonnes
Engines: Gardner, Cummins, Rolls-Royce, Caterpillar
Cab/bonnet layout: Forward control

The S10 range — consisting of the S104 four-wheeler, S106 six-wheeler and S108 eight-wheeler — was announced shortly before the old company finally folded, and has been refined mechanically by Paccar which added the option of Caterpillar engines in 1983. The tilt cab profile is slightly squarer than its predecessor, and single-piece windscreen models have a flatter screen. The Foden moulding has become progressively smaller.

Below left:
Two-piece windscreen and large single headlamps identify a Foden S90-cabbed Haulmaster tractive unit.

Above:
The higher specification S95-cabbed Foden Fleetmaster has a single-piece windscreen and twin headlamps.

Right:
An S10-cab Foden Fleetmaster converted into a 6×2 tractive unit with a lifting axle. Foden-built six-wheel tractive units are all 6×4.

Right:
A newer Foden S108 tipper with a shallower grille design and a smaller Foden kite logo. This one is powered by a 320hp Gardner 6LYT engine.

Ford

Ford's British truck manufacturing business grew up in the 1950s, culminating in its move from the main centre of operations at Dagenham, Essex, to a purpose-built factory at Langley, Buckinghamshire. It has been a consistent market leader in the market for trucks over 3.5 tonnes, but Leyland overtook it from the beginning of 1986. It has pulled out of some of the markets it used to serve, and is stopping making its own axles. From July 1986, its truck business has effectively been controlled by Iveco in a jointly-owned company, Iveco Ford Truck.

A-Series

Country of origin: England
Weight range: 3.5 to 6 tonnes
Engines: Ford petrol or diesel
Cab/bonnet layout: Normal control

The A-Series light truck, plugging the gap between the Transit van and D-Series truck, was built from 1973 to 1983. Its cab design has many parts in common with the Transit, notably the doors, but it sits higher off the ground. An integral van was available for a time in the 1970s, but failed to sell well. Ultimately, the A-Series lost out to the Dodge 50 in this small market.

Above:
A box van-bodied Ford A-Series chassis/cab with its cab developed from the Transit van. The bonnet and grille are of a design exclusive to the A-Series.

Right:
The short-lived Willenhall-bodied Ford A-Series integral van has a taller, flatter windscreen with quarterlights. It shares the bonnet assembly of the chassis/cab.

Above:
An earlier model Ford D-Series with white fluted grille wrapping around as far as the cab doors. It also has the Ford name spelt out on the grille. Peter Rowlands

Below:
A later Ford D-Series with a matt black grille and Ford name on an oval badge.

D-Series

Country of origin: England
Weight range: 5.9 to 28 tonnes
Engines: Ford, Cummins, Perkins
Cab/bonnet layout: Forward control

Probably Ford's most successful British truck ever, the D-Series was built from 1965 to 1981. The tilt cab is square, but with a raked windscreen and the inevitable stepped down side quarterlights. It was built in 5.9- to 28-tonne versions, with Ford engines, inclined to nearside, on the lighter models, and Cummins or Perkins engines on the heavier models which may also be identified by their wider mudguards.

H-Series Transcontinental

Country of origin: Netherlands, England
Weight range: 32.5 to 44 tonnes
Engines: Cummins
Cab/bonnet layout: Forward control

Like Bedford and Dodge, Ford was keen to gain a slice of an expected upsurge in demand for heavyweight international haulage vehicles. Rather than design a vehicle from scratch, it brought together proven components which it assembled at its Amsterdam plant to make the Transcontinental 44-tonner from 1975. The cab came from Berliet (later Renault), engines from Cummins, gearboxes from Fuller and axles from Rockwell. After the Amsterdam plant was closed, assembly was moved to the Foden factory at Sandbach, where they were made under contract from 1982 until production ceased at the end of the following year. Renault had the cabs painted at the Karrier plant in Dunstable before delivering them to Sandbach.

Below:
A Ford Transcontinental tractive unit pulling a tri-axle tilt semi-trailer. Earlier models had white grilles and the Ford name spelt out across the front.

Cargo

Country of origin: England
Weight range: 6 to 38 tonnes
Engines: Ford, Cummins, Perkins, Deutz
Cab/bonnet layout: Forward control

The Cargo was launched in 1981 to replace the D-Series and has been extended up the weight range to include 32.5- and 38-tonne tractive units, a move which goes a little way towards making up for the withdrawal of the Transcontinental. The lower weight models have air cooled Deutz engines. The cab has all the hallmarks of Ford's design flair. Close attention was paid to aerodynamics and the cab flares out at the back to assist air flow. The quarterlights are much deeper than on other models, in order to give greater kerbside visibility when manoeuvring. The model designation appears on a plastic panel behind the quarterlight, types ranging from 0609 (6-tonner, 88hp) to 3824 (38-tonner, 249hp).

Above:
A 7.5-tonne Ford Cargo 0811 with 114hp engine and glass-carrying body. The model number on the Cargo is displayed level with the wing mirror bracket, in the deep quarterlight.

Below:
A heavier Ford Cargo, a 24-tonne 6×4 2417 with 180hp Perkins V8-540 engine. This one has a diesel-powered crane to load roofing tiles.

Guy

Guy Motors was independent until it went bankrupt in 1960. The Wolverhampton-based business was acquired by Jaguar the following year and in 1968 became part of the newly created British Leyland Motor Corporation. It maintained its identity for some years afterwards, but gradually took on the manufacture of other Leyland trucks, latterly Landtrain export models.

Big J

Country of origin: England
Weight range: 16 to 32.5 tonnes
Engines: Cummins, Gardner, Rolls-Royce, Leyland, AEC
Cab/bonnet layout: Forward control

The 16- to 32-ton Big J, launched in September 1964, was Guy's last design of home market truck. The cab was built by Motor Panels, to a design similar to that used by Seddon, but with a more elaborate radiator and headlight arrangement. Early models have an essentially horizontal radiator grille, later models a larger more upright design. Big Js were fitted with Cummins, Gardner, Rolls-Royce, Leyland and AEC engines. Production ceased in 1976.

Hino

Japanese vehicle manufacturers are bound by a so-called 'gentlemen's agreement' with Britain's Society of Motor Manufacturers and Traders not to sell goods vehicles over 3.5 tonnes GVW on the British market. Despite that, the products of Hino Motors, the world's second largest manufacturer of trucks of over 7 tonnes GVW (after Mercedes-Benz) gained a toehold on the British market in 1980. It achieved this as it already had gained a dominant share of the Irish Republic's truck market by undertaking final assembly of the trucks at the Dublin plant of a former Guy assembler, J. Harris (Assemblers) Ltd. An Irish-managed company, HCV Motor Vehicle Distributors, started importing trucks to Britain from Dublin through a base at Warrington. The successes in Ireland have not yet been matched in Britain, where operators have demanded a more sophisticated product. Hino is part-owned by Toyota and is pronounced 'Hee-no'.

HE/ZM

Country of origin: Japan
Weight range: 24 to 32.5 tonnes
Engines: Hino, Cummins
Cab/bonnet layout: Forward control

The two basic models imported to Britain from 1980 share the same cab, but are otherwise very different. The HE336 tractive unit is designed for 32.5-tonne operation and is fitted with either a 243hp six-cylinder or 320hp V8 Hino engine, although HCV has also experimented with a Cummins engine to make the model more acceptable to British operators. The ZM six- or eight-wheeler, with 243hp Hino engine, has proved a more popular model in Britain, especially for tipper work. The cab is dated by the standards of competitors' products, and sits high on the HE with fluted panelling behind the cab door, above the wheel, where the wheel would be on a lighter model. It has a large, horizontally-slatted grille, with twin headlamps either side. On the ZM, the cab is lower, with the door fitting around the front wheel, and the grille is of a more elaborate, horizontal pattern which incorporates the twin headlamp. All have the winged Hino motif above the grille. Some Hinos have three green lights on the cab roof, a Japanese feature to show the speed at which the truck is running.

Left: *An earlier model Guy Big J8 eight-wheel tipper.*

Below left: *A later model Guy Big J4T tractive unit with larger grille.* Peter Rowlands

Below: *A Hino HE336 tractive unit.* Peter Rowlands

Above: *A Hino ZM eight-wheel tipper.* Peter Rowlands

SH/FS/KY

Country of origin: Japan
Weight range: 24 to 38 tonnes
Engines: Hino, Cummins
Cab/bonnet layout: Forward control

Hino launched a new range of trucks in 1982 as replacement for HE and ZM, but type approval problems have delayed their launch until 1986. The SH273 tractive units, FS six-wheeler and KY eight-wheeler share many of the mechanical components of the older models, but have a more modern and lower cab. It has a more rounded profile, with doors on all models fitting around the front wheels. The SH has a rectangular grille influenced by its predecessor's, while the six- and eight-wheelers have a more horizontal design.

Below:
The new generation of Hino is represented by the SH273 tractive unit. The lights under the operator's nameboard illuminate as the truck attains higher speeds.
Commercial Motor

Iveco

The Industrial Vehicles Corporation — Iveco for short — is the Amsterdam-based, English language commercial vehicle wing of Fiat, the Italian automotive giant. It was formed in 1975 by amalgamating Fiat's then 72-year-old truck-making business, and its subsidiaries OM and French-based Unic with Magirus Deutz, the commercial vehicle subsidiary of a West German engineering group, Klöckner Humboldt Deutz (KHD). KHD held a 20% stake in Iveco until 1980, when it sold its shareholding to Fiat, but it continued to supply an albeit diminishing number of Deutz engines to the group. The Deutz name was dropped from Magirus models after that, but from 1982 the Iveco name has taken precedence on all models. To contain costs, the former Unic plant at Trappes, near Paris, was closed in 1984. It gained effective control of Ford's UK truck business in July 1986.

Iveco Z-range/Fiat OM/Magirus 90D

Country of origin: Italy
Weight range: 5.5 to 7.5 tonnes
Engines: OM, Iveco, Deutz
Cab/bonnet layout: Forward control

Above:
A Fiat OM55 chassis/cab with pantechnicon body and earlier style of grille with vertical slats.

The light trucks sold since 1979 as the Iveco Z-range first came to Britain in 1973 when Fiat began importing trucks from Italy. They are built at the OM factory at Brescia, and for the British market were marketed as the Fiat OM55 5.5-tonner and OM75 7.5-tonner, both being powered by 85hp OM diesel engines. When Iveco rationalised its ranges to offer Fiat's water-cooled engines in Magirus models and air-cooled Deutz engines in Fiat models, a four-cylinder Deutz engine was offered in the Brescia range and sold as the Magirus Deutz 90D5.6FL 5.6-ton or 90D7.5FL 7.5-ton. When it became the Z-range, Fiat's 96hp diesel became standard and the Fiat models were redesignated 60F10 (5.6-ton) and 79F10 (7.5-ton); the Magirus models became the 90M6.0FL and 90M7.9FV. By 1985, the Iveco-badged models were sold in Britain in three forms, the 06.10 6-tonner and 79.10 7.5-tonners with 94hp engines and the 79.14 7.5-tonner with 135hp engine. From its introduction to Britain in 1973, this range has been available both as a chassis/cab and as an integral van. Both have a generally square cab profile with a shallow grille and raked windscreen. Vans have a taller windscreen which dwarfs the cab door windows. Later vans have a tall window, to the same height as the windscreen, fitted behind the nearside cab door; earlier ones have a shallow window above the cab doors.

Above:
An Iveco 60.10 integral van with the later style of grille and with the curious window effect created by the tall window behind the nearside door, to remove a blindspot. It has the same cab doors as the chassis/cab.

Iveco/Magirus modular cab models

Country of origin: West Germany
Weight range: 30 to 32.5 tonnes
Engines: Deutz
Cab/bonnet layout: Forward control

Magirus Deutz assembled trucks in Britain, at Winsford, Cheshire (later the Iveco UK headquarters), in the late-1960s, using the low modular cab in production in West Germany in 1963. Economics soon swung in favour of importing complete vehicles from the main factory at Ulm. Tractive units and rigid vehicles — tippers mainly — have been sold in Britain, but the cab was replaced by the Iveco cab on tractive units by 1979 and on tippers in 1986. All of these vehicles have Deutz engines. There is a kerbside window in the nearside door.

Left:
A Magirus Deutz 310 tractive unit with naturally aspirated V10 Deutz engine and the 1963 modular cab.

Right:
A Fiat I59NC17 16-tonne rigid lorry used to carry refrigerated goods. It has the all-steel tilt-cab first built in 1970.
Peter Rowlands

Above:
The long-lived Magirus Deutz 232D30FK 8×4 tipper with naturally aspirated Deutz V8 diesel. The rocket-like Magirus logo on the grille is a representation of Ulm Minster, the principal landmark of Magirus's home town.

Iveco/Fiat/Magirus standard cab models

Country of origin: Italy, West Germany, France
Weight range: 11.2 to 44 tonnes
Engines: Fiat, Deutz, Iveco
Cab/bonnet layout: Forward control

Fiat developed an all-steel tilt cab for heavier vehicles which was launched in 1970, and which has been available in Britain since 1974. It has been fitted to Magirus vehicles since 1978, the same year as the round-edged Fiat grille was replaced by a horizontally-slatted Iveco design. Newer models have a large roof-mounted wind deflector to aid fuel consumption when driving against strong winds. Models currently available in Britain range from the 109.14 11.2-tonne with 135hp engine to the 190.42 44-tonne tractive unit with 420hp turbocharged V8 engine. Heavier models use a wider version of the cab.

Above:
An Iveco 190.30T tractive unit with 304hp turbocharged water-cooled engine and roof-mounted wind deflector.

Iveco/Magirus bonneted range

Country of origin: West Germany
Weight range: 19 to 26 tonnes
Engines: Deutz
Cab/bonnet layout: Normal control

Iveco sells on/off-road Magirus-designed tippers on the British market with a square cab, bonnet and large, square grille. The current range is the four-wheel-drive 190.25ANW 19-tonner with eight-cylinder 256hp Deutz engine, the 260.25AN 26-tonne 6×4 model, and the six-wheel-drive 260.25 26-tonner.

Below:
A 1979 model Magirus Deutz 232D24K tipper with 228hp V8 air-cooled diesel.

Karrier

See Dodge

Leyland

The nucleus of the business which trades today as Leyland Trucks (part of Leyland Vehicles and, in turn, part of the British Leyland (BL) Group) was founded in 1896 as the Lancashire Steam Motor Co and became Leyland Motors in 1907. Today it is still based at Leyland, Lancashire and is owned by the British government, but its truck-building origins are more complex. It first expanded to take over Albion Motors of Glasgow in 1951 and Scammell Lorries of Watford in 1955, and in 1962 it bought the Southall, West London-based AEC business. It reached its zenith six years later when the British Leyland Motor Corporation was created by merging Leyland and British Motor Holdings. With BMH came the British Motor Corporation (BMC) range of Austin and Morris trucks (built mainly at Bathgate, West Lothian but also at a Birmingham van factory) and Guy Motors, the Jaguar subsidiary based in Wolverhampton. It built a new assembly plant at Leyland, which opened in 1979, and has gradually closed down most of the other plants. Southall closed in 1979, then Wolverhampton, and Bathgate (which took over truck production from Albion and heavy van production from Birmingham) was run down to close finally in 1986. That has left Albion as the company's axle plant and Scammell building specialist vehicles, some of them badged as Leylands. Its engine building has also been reduced to two ranges, the 400 and TL11 built at Leyland, and their long-term future looks doubtful. Leyland has been steadily regaining its share of the British truck market, and has increased its exports to Europe, although it is still primarily a British Commonwealth exporter. It also has an Indian associate Ashok Leyland.

Leyland/Albion LAD range

Country of origin: England, Scotland
Weight range: 10 to 24 tonnes
Engines: Leyland
Cab/bonnet layout: Forward control

Above:
Typical of late LAD-cabbed models is this Albion Reiver with ready-mixed-concrete mixer body.

A common design of Motor Panels cab, most of which were built from steel although a short-lived glass fibre version appeared in the early 1960s, was used by Leyland, Albion and Dodge Brothers (Britain) from July 1958 and remained the principal Albion truck cab until 1972. It is rounded with the front dash bulging out in two stages. The single-piece windscreen and cab door windows are all level; the grille is in two horizontally-slatted sections with the headlamps set in triangular mouldings either side of the lower half; and the maker's name is displayed between the two grille sections. Leyland used the LAD cab latterly on its Bear six-wheel tipper/mixer, while Albion retained it for its Chieftain 10- to 13-ton, Clydesdale 14- to 16-ton, and Reiver 21- to 24-ton ranges.

Leyland/Albion/AEC Ergomatic range

Country of origin: England, Scotland
Weight range: 16 to 32.5 tonnes
Engines: Leyland, AEC
Cab/bonnet layout: Forward control

Leyland's first production tilt cab, designed to make the driver's and mechanic's life easier (using ergonomics — the study of people in their working environment) was introduced in 1964 as the Sankey (later GKN)-built Ergomatic cab. It is a square design with a deep windscreen, full-width grille, and separate quarterlight and main windows on the cab doors. The quarterlight is the same depth as the windscreen. Leyland kept it in production longest, until the T45 range came on stream, and fitted it on Super Comet 16-tonners, Retriever and Hippo 22-tonners, Bison and Super Buffalo 24-tonners, Super Hippo and Octopus 30-tonne eight-wheelers, and Beaver, Lynx and Buffalo tractive units. Leyland's fixed-head 500-Series engine of 1968 (the source of many lost orders for the company in the 1970s) was fitted in Lynx, Buffalo, Bison, Octopus and Super Buffalo models, although the TL11 and AEC-designed L12 were offered in the Buffalo (TL11) and Octopus (L12) by 1979. The grille was redesigned on later models. Albion used the same

Below:
A Leyland Beaver 32.5-tonne tractive unit with the original grille style of the Ergomatic-cabbed models. Peter Rowlands

Top right:
A 500-Series-engined Leyland Lynx milk tanker with the second version of the Ergomatic cab grille squared off and with the Leyland name displayed at the top.

Centre right:
The third and final version of the Ergomatic cab's grille is painted rather than finished in chrome and has fewer and broader horizontal slats. The Leyland name is bigger. This is a Bison 2.

Bottom right:
Albion versions of the Ergomatic range have that company's sunrise name badge at the top of the grille and the supplementary thistle-on-saltire badge beneath the windscreen. This is a Super Clydesdale tractive unit.

GAVIN BERTRAM
LEYLAND
HSY 724G

DRG
Hales Containers
Hales
WASTEATER
LEYLAND
Chesham 772681
XKX 188X

D.E. HINES
STREETLY
Streetly
1341
Albion
24
XRF 858C

cab on its Super Clydesdale 16-ton and Super Reiver 18- to 22-ton models until 1972. AEC used it on its Mercury 16-tonner, Marshal, Marshal Major and Mammoth Major six- and eight-wheelers, and Mandator tractive units, the last of which were built in 1977/78.

Below:
An AEC Mandator tractive unit with that company's blue triangle logo mounted beneath the windscreen.

Marathon

Country of origin: England
Weight range: 32.5 to 44 tonnes
Engines: Leyland (AEC), Cummins, Rolls-Royce
Cab/bonnet layout: Forward control

The Marathon 32.5- to 44-tonner, as the list of model names above suggests, was developed by AEC, which built most of them. It was Leyland's answer to the growing demand for international haulage vehicles, and uses a higher cab based on the Ergomatic design, but with a secondary, lower grille with nine rectangular apertures flanked either side by three dummy apertures, and with shallow quarterlights incorporated in the single door windows. Standard engine was the AEC-designed TL12, but Rolls-Royce and Cummins engines were also offered. It was launched in August 1973 and was superseded in 1980, with production latterly being undertaken by Scammell. Guy built some earlier models.

Leyland/BMC/Austin/Morris G-cab range

Country of origin: Scotland
Weight range: 6.6 to 24 tonnes
Engines: BMC, Leyland, Perkins
Cab/bonnet layout: Forward control

Bathgate-built G-cab tilt-cab trucks have been around since the FJ-range was launched by BMC in 1964. It is very much a product of that time, having a slightly raked one-piece windscreen and cab door with deeper quarterlights level with the depth of the windscreen. Until 1970, three basic models were built, the 1968 Laird 9.6- to 12-tonner, the Boxer 14.5-tonner with Perkins six-cylinder engine, and the Mastiff 16- to 24-tonner with Perkins V8 engine. From 1970, when the range was renamed Leyland, the Terrier 6.6- to 9.6-tonner was introduced, and the Boxer range was extended to start at 10 tonnes (with a BMC engine) in place of the Laird. In 1972, Albion started fitting the cab (in place of the LAD and Ergomatic cabs) to its Chieftain, Clydesdale and Reiver models which, henceforth, were badged as Leylands and were built latterly at Bathgate. Earlier models have single-piece grilles with horizontal slats and V-shaped vertical divisions. From 1972, the design was revised with a larger Leyland name beneath the windscreen, a horizontal grille with a Leyland roundel in the centre, and a lower row of eight plainer apertures. This was revised again in 1980 when the upper grille and badge areas became matt black. Production was run down until 1984, when the Terrier was dropped.

Below left:
A line of Leyland Marathon tractive units on dock work hauling from Tilbury.

Below:
A BMC-badged Laird and (left) a Leyland-badged Boxer display the different styles of grille used on the G-cab range over the years. George Brown

LEYLAND
41

LEYLAND
B.Birch & Sons
Haulage
LINDALE
2775
OEC 64P

LEYLAND
TERRIER
BOROUGH OF HAVANT
LPX 724Y

Left:
A Leyland Chieftain with the 1972-style grille and painted in Ripponden and District Motors' traditional livery.

Centre left:
Extra Leyland badges are fitted on the grille of this Leyland Clydesdale quarry tipper in use in South Cumbria.

Bottom left:
A Leyland Terrier operated by the Borough of Havant, showing the black grille and Leyland name. Its cab has been extended to accommodate additional crew.

Leyland/BMC/Austin/Morris WF

Country of origin: England, Scotland
Weight range: 3.6 to 9 tonnes
Engines: BMC diesel or petrol
Cab/bonnet layout: Normal control

The bonneted WF, although sold latterly only as an export truck, was still available to home market customers as late as 1974 as a 3.6- to 9-tonner. It first appeared with twin headlamps and single-piece windscreen in 1964.

Above:
A bonneted Austin WF horsebox. The 1964 design of this model was developed from an earlier style with two-piece windscreen. George Brown

Leyland/BMC/Austin/Morris FG

Country of origin: England, Scotland
Weight range: 3.6 to 9 tonnes
Engines: BMC diesel or petrol
Cab/bonnet layout: Forward control

BMC called in London University's Professor G. C. Drew to undertake ergonomic research on the urban delivery van which was launched in 1959 as the FG. Its most distinctive features were the cab doors which are behind the driver at an angle of 45° to the sides, and which hinge at the back. This means the vehicle may be driven with the doors open for quick exit and entry on regular stops. The front slopes back sharply, leaving space for very short windows at the sides. Additional windows are fitted below the windscreen, either side of the grille, for kerbside visibility. The 3.6- to 9-tonne FG was especially popular as a baker's van and remained in production until 1981.

Above:
The largest FG model is the 900FG 9.1-tonner, seen here badged as an Austin. The bonnet and radiator protrude to accommodate a 5.1-litre six-cylinder diesel engine.

Left:
More typical of the FGs around is this Leyland-badged dropside lorry operated by a potato merchant. George Brown

Leyland/BMC/Austin/Morris EA

Country of origin: England, Scotland
Weight range: 3.5 to 4.4 tonnes
Engines: BMC diesel or petrol
Cab/bonnet layout: Forward control

The 3.5- to 4.4-tonne EA, production of which moved from the Midlands to Scotland by 1974, was built from 1968 to 1981. It replaced the long-running BMC LD van beloved of the Post Office, and it was the Post Office again which became a loyal buyer of the EA. It has a raked front with a single-piece curved windscreen and horizontally slatted grille. The sides are flat, with sliding cab doors on vans, hinged ones on trucks. Leyland deserted this market with the demise of the EA, leaving it to Freight Rover, BL's van subsidiary based in Birmingham.

Left:
A Leyland EA van operated by East Midlands Gas. The grille outline bears a family resemblance to the original style of G-cab trucks.

Right:
Two examples of Leyland T45 trucks with the wider cab. The articulated outfit is pulled by a Roadtrain tractive unit, while the eight-wheeler is a Scammell-built Constructor. Both have Rolls-Royce engines.

T45 range

Country of origin: England
Weight range: 11 to 65 tonnes
Engines: Leyland, Perkins, Cummins, Gardner, Rolls-Royce, Daf
Cab/bonnet layout: Forward control

The rationalised range with which Leyland was to compete in the 1980s was developed with the code name T45 which became so well known that it has been retained for some of Leyland's sales efforts. Production — much delayed as final development work (some in association with the then nationalised British Road Services) was completed — began in 1980 with the launch of the Roadtrain tractive unit. Since then, it has been expanded to a range from 11 to 65 tonnes, all distinguished by a Motor Panels cab (designated C40) styled exclusively for Leyland by Ogle Design with a 'soft' low profile intended to make them look less aggressive than their Ergomatic predecessors. Two versions of the cab are used — a wide one running to the full width of the mudguards with vertical slats on the front dash panel and twin headlamps in the front bumper, and a narrow one with protruding mudguards, a plain front dash panel, and single headlamps. All have cab door windows which slope gently downwards to the front, in line with the slightly raked windscreen which sits above a black mock windscreen extension upon which the Leyland name is displayed. The cab tucks in at wheel level and the model name and trafficator lights appear on a shallow panel between the cab bottom, air intake and front bumper. The 11- to 16-tonne models are called Freighter and have narrow cabs and Leyland engines (Bathgate-built 5.7-litre 98 Series in most, 400 Series 6.5-litre units in 16.13, 16.15 and 16.17 16-tonners with 135hp, 154hp and 172hp engines). Next up the weight range is the six-wheel 24-tonne Constructor with narrow cab and choice of 154hp or 180hp 400 Series engine (models 24.15 and 24.17) or the 209hp TL11 11.1-litre unit (24.21). Eight-wheel 30-tonners, also called Constructor, are built by Scammell and have wide cabs and a choice of TL11, Cummins L10, Gardner or Rolls-Royce engines. Lightweight tractive units for 20- to 35-tonne operation are called Cruiser and use the narrow cab and Leyland engines (either the 400 Series for 20- to 24-tonne 16.15 and 16.17 models or the TL11 for 24.4- to 35-tonne work). The Roadtrain 32.5- to 40-tonne 4×2 was offered initially only with the Marathon's TL12 engine, but Rolls-Royce and Cummins options followed and the Rolls-Royce became standard after production of the TL12 ceased. The 6×2 Roadtrain, built by Scammell, uses a 14-litre Cummins engine. There also is a 6×4 Cummins-engined Roadtrain for operation at up to 65 tonnes. All Roadtrains use the wide cab.

Left:
Scammell's identity is stamped on the 6×2 Roadtrain 20.32 with 14-litre Cummins engine. Although it carries the Leyland name beneath the windscreen, Scammell's name appears larger than Roadtrain, above the nearside headlamps.

Below:
An example of the narrower C40 cab on a Cruiser tractive unit. This is a 16.23 32.5-tonne unit fitted with 224hp Leyland TL11 engine.

Roadrunner

Country of origin: England
Weight range: 6.2 to 10 tonnes
Engines: Leyland, Cummins
Cab/bonnet layout: Forward control

Leyland's new range was completed in 1984 with the launch of the Roadrunner 6.2- to 10-tonner which replaced the Terrier and, thanks to an advertising campaign using a French stunt driver, promoted as 'the toughest truck on two wheels'. It uses another Motor Panels/Ogle cab (the C44) which owes much to the larger C40, and shares the same doors. It sits lower and differs below the windscreen by having a nearside parking window upon which the Leyland name is displayed, and has a shallow horizontally-slatted grille with square headlights and trafficators either side. The bumper is devoid of any lights. It was launched with the 98 Series engine, but it was replaced by the Cummins B Series (badged Leyland 300) after the Bathgate engine plant closed in 1986.

Below:
A Leyland Roadrunner 8.12 7.5-tonne 112hp model with a curtain-sided body.

Magirus Deutz

See Iveco

MAN-VW

Maschinenfabrik Augsburg-Nurnbürg — MAN to the world at large — can trace its origins to the genesis of the modern lorry. It made its first diesel engine before the end of the last century and was building its first diesel-engined lorries in the 1920s. It started selling trucks in Britain in January 1974 and now sells them through MAN-VW Trucks and Bus, a division of the Lonrho-owned Volkswagen/Audi car sales company based at Milton Keynes, from its own premises in Swindon. The Volkswagen connection is no accident, as a jointly developed range of medium weight trucks is produced by the two companies. Although part of a larger industrial group, MAN is still a much smaller West German manufacturer than Mercedes-Benz and is likely to need to collaborate with another manufacturer to survive. The possibility of a takeover by General Motors was raised, then dropped, in the 1980s.

MAN DHK range

Country of origin: West Germany
Weight range: 16 to 32 tonnes
Engines: MAN
Cab/bonnet layout: Semi-forward control

The semi-forward control DHK range tipper is a mid-1960s design identifiable by its rounded cab, the overhanging engine compartment ahead of the front axle, and the smoke stack running from the offside of the engine compartment to the cab roof. They are available in conventional and all-wheel-drive versions, the latter being coded DHAK. Three weight ranges are available, the 16-tonne 16.240, the 26-tonne 26.240 and the 32-tonne 32.240. All have 237hp engines.

Above:
A semi-forward control MAN 32.240DHK tipper on site work in Renfrewshire. The roof exhaust minimises the risk of it being damaged in rough conditions. George Brown

MAN F range

Country of origin: West Germany
Weight range: 16 to 58.7 tonnes
Engines: MAN
Cab/bonnet layout: Forward control

The forward control MAN F8 range is sold in Britain from 16-tonne distribution lorry to 58.7-tonne heavy haulage tractor. It uses a French-designed cab developed by Saviem at the time when the two manufacturers had a close working partnership. The distinguishing features are the rectangular, chrome-surrounded grille and cab windows with a shallow non-opening section at the top. Smallest in the range is the 16.170F 16.3-tonner with 168hp engine; eight-wheelers are the 30.240 and 30.281 30.5-tonners with 237hp and 276hp engines respectively; tractive units are the 16.240 (up to 38 tonnes with 237hp engine), 16.281 (up to 44 tonnes with 276hp engine), 16.321 (up to 44 tonnes with 315hp engine), and 19.361 (up to 44 tonnes with 356hp engine); and for heavy haulage work the heaviest are the 20.321 (up to 50 tonnes with 315hp engine) and the 20.361 (up to 50.8 tonnes with 356hp engine). All engines are built by MAN.

Below left:
A MAN 30.240VF 8×4 fitted with a Saviem day cab.

Above:
Top of MAN's British range is the 22.361FVLTS 6×2 twin-steer tractive unit with air suspension on its second and third axles. The longer window behind the cab door indicates a sleeper cab.

MAN F90 range

Country of origin: West Germany
Weight range: 16 to 58.7 tonnes
Engines: MAN
Cab/bonnet layout: Forward control

Above:
The smoother lines of the MAN F90 cab are achieved partly by greater use of plastics.

Right:
The different cab door design of the F90 on an MAN 19.362 tractive unit.

A two-year programme to replace the 25-year-old F8-cabbed range began in 1986, starting with tractive units and working down to 16-tonners. The F90 cab, unlike its French-designed predecessor, is designed and built entirely by MAN. The rectangular grille preserves a family identity, but all the cab pressings are different and the doors have a slight hint of Mercedes, with a slightly deeper quarterlight. It is 140mm wider than the F8, although the design allows for narrower cabs. The first British market models, the 19.362 (360hp) and 16.321 (330hp) 4×2 tractive units, have 12-litre turbocharged and charge-cooled MAN diesels and are expected to arrive here in February 1987 to replace the 19.361 and 19.332. A smaller version of the F90 is likely to replace the Volkswagen cab on the MT at a later date.

MAN-VW MT range

Country of origin: West Germany
Weight range: 6.5 to 10 tonnes
Engines: MAN
Cab/bonnet layout: Forward control

Above:
A MAN-VW MT range curtain-sided light truck. The grille badge matches the two firms' identities. Alan Millar

The MT range was launched in 1979 and plugs the 6.5- to 10-tonne gap between Volkswagen's LT van range and MAN's F range. Essentially, the MT is a marriage of MAN mechanical units to a modified version of the LT's cab and a Volkswagen gearbox. It sits higher off the ground than the LT and has a MAN-style rectangular grille. The 6.5- and 7.5-tonne MT6.90 and MT8.90 use a 90hp MAN four-cylinder diesel engine, while the 7.5-tonne, 9-tonne and 10-tonne MT8.136, MT9.136 and MT10.136 have a six-cylinder MAN 136hp diesel.

Mercedes-Benz

Mercedes-Benz, apart from being the model name of Daimler-Benz and credited with production of the first motor car, is one of the world's largest truck builders. It has been selling lorries, on and off, in Britain for a very long time and imported the first diesel-engined lorries to Britain in 1928. By 1985, it had overtaken Dodge and Bedford to become the third best-selling make of truck over 3.5 tonnes. Like MAN and Scania, its British sales operation is run from Milton Keynes.

LP range

Country of origin: West Germany
Weight range: 8.5 to 32.5 tonnes
Engines: Mercedes-Benz
Cab/bonnet layout: Forward control

Below:
The Mercedes-Benz LPS1319 tractive unit is a lighter but more powerful version of the LPS1418. It is shown here coupled to a Hoynor car transporter semi-trailer.

Bottom:
At the lighter end of the LP range is the 1113 11-tonner with 125hp engine. In common with other Mercedes models, it has spray deflectors mounted either side of the grille.

The LP range Mercedes, available in Britain from 8.5-tonne LP809 to 32.5-tonne LPS1418 tractive unit, first appeared in 1965 and remained in 8.5- to 11-tonne form until 1984. The tractive unit and 2419 tipper were replaced by Mercedes' new generation trucks in 1974. It has a square cab with a slightly curved one-piece windscreen slightly taller than the cab door windows. The grille is fairly shallow and sits above the bumper, upon which the headlamps are mounted. The Mercedes three-pointed star sits in the middle of the grille. On the lighter models, the wheels are set forward, but they are behind the cab doors on the tractive unit.

L508/608

Country of origin: West Germany
Weight range: 3.5 to 5.2 tonnes
Engines: Mercedes-Benz
Cab/bonnet layout: Forward control

The forward control L508 and L608 light truck is another mid-1960s Mercedes which has enjoyed a long production run, from 1967 to replacement in mid-1986. The L508 is a 3.5- to 5.2-tonner, the L608 a 5.7- to 6.4-tonner. They are available as vans or chassis/cabs and all have four-cylinder 85hp Mercedes diesel engines. The windscreen is a three-piece design and the hinged door is behind the front axle.

Below:
A Mercedes-Benz L608D box van being used for door-to-door deliveries of frozen foods.

T2 range

Country of origin: West Germany
Weight range: 3.5 to 7.5 tonnes
Engines: Mercedes-Benz
Cab/bonnet layout: Normal control

The 1986 successor to the L508/608 range — code-named T2 and (earlier) LN1 — is built in a weight range from 3.5 to 7.5 tonnes. It retains its predecessor's bonnet layout, but its cab is developed from that on the heavier LN2 range. On chassis/cabs, the cab is identical; on integral vans, it has a deeper windscreen and an extra, horizontal window at the top of the door. Six models are built: the 507D (71hp, 3.5 to 4.6 tonnes); 609D (88hp, 3.5 to 5.6 tonnes); 709D (88hp, 5.9 to 6.6 tonnes); 711D (114hp, 6.6 tonnes); 809D (88hp, 7.5 tonnes); and 811D (114hp, 7.5 tonnes).

Top:
The common cabs of the LN2 and T2 Mercedes are exemplified by this line-up of (left to right) an LN2 814, a T2 811D and a 309D model from the Bremen van range.

Above:
The higher windscreen and cab doors of the T2 integral van show clearly on this 507D model.

'New generation'

Country of origin: West Germany
Weight range: 13.3 to 38 tonnes
Engines: Mercedes-Benz
Cab/bonnet layout: Forward control

The so-called 'new generation' Mercedes range, styled to lessen their visual impact on the environment, first appeared in 1974 and are now available in Britain as vehicles from 13.3-tonners to 38-tonne tractive units. It is a curved design with raked windscreen and a front dash which is also raked towards the bottom. The cab door windows have a deeper quarterlight which is level with the windscreen. The full-width grille has the star in the middle. The 1213 13-tonners use a 125hp Mercedes six-cylinder engine, 1617 16-tonners and 24.4-tonne tractive units have a 168hp six-cylinder engine, 1625 16-tonne drawbar units 3025 eight-wheeled tippers and 38-tonne tractive units have a 247hp V8 engine, and 1621 32.5-tonne tractive units and 2421 24-tonners have a 201hp V6 engine; V8s are also fitted in the other 38-tonners, the 1628 4×2 (276hp), the 1633 4×2 (325hp), the 2025 6×2 (247hp), 2028 6×2 (276hp) and the 2033 6×2 (325hp).

Below:
One of the smaller vehicles with the Mercedes-Benz 'new generation' cab is the 1213 13-tonner, seen here as a brewery delivery truck.

Bottom:
A Mercedes-Benz 2028LS 6×2 tractive unit coupled to a curtain-sided Tautliner semi-trailer.

LN2 range

Country of origin: West Germany
Weight range: 7.5 to 13 tonnes
Engines: Mercedes-Benz
Cab/bonnet layout: Forward control

The replacements for the LP lightweights appeared in 1984, initially in 7.5-tonne and 11-tonne form with a choice of 88hp (model 809) or 134hp (model 814) in the 7.5-tonner and the 134hp engine in the 11-tonne 1114. A 13-tonner was added at the end of 1985. The design is influenced by the 'new generation' models, with raked windscreen and front dash, and the cab door windows slope towards the front to end up in line with the full depth of the windscreen. Unlike its predecessor, the front axle is set back from the front.

Below:
The squarer lines of the LN2 range compares with a 'new generation' Mercedes-Benz 1617K on the right. The LN2 is an 814 in a London area tipper rental fleet.

Morris

See Leyland

Pegaso

Country of origin: Spain
Weight range: Not sold in Britain
Engines: Pegaso
Cab/bonnet layout: Forward control

Pegaso is the heavy truck brand name used by Empresa Nacional de Autocamiones SA (Enasa), the Spanish state-owned commercial vehicle manufacturer which also makes Sava vans. At one time, it was part-owned by Leyland and used some Leyland engines and other components in its vehicles. International Harvester bought into the company in 1980 with a view to establishing a jointly owned engine plant in Spain, but IH's financial troubles killed off that project and led Enasa to end up buying Seddon Atkinson, IH's British truck manufacturing subsidiary, in 1984. Enasa is engaged in joint development of a cab with Daf, through a company called Cabtech. Although the company does not sell trucks in Britain, they are a familiar sight on British roads on international journeys from Spain. The current generation of Pegasos dates from 1972, when the square, ribbed side-tilt cab was introduced. It has large grille intakes and the cab door windows have slightly deeper quarterlights in line with the windscreen.

Below:
Three examples of the latest version of Pegaso's truck range. Older models have a cruder grille with large open intakes.

Renault

Renault Vehicules Industriels is the commercial vehicle wing of Régie Renault, the French state-owned motor group. It began to take shape in 1955 when Renault took over the Somua and Latil businesses and merged them into Saviem (SA des Vehicules et Equipments Mécaniques), a company which forged close technical links with MAN in the 1960s. In 1975, it was expanded further by the acquisition of Berliet, Citroën's commercial vehicle subsidiary (since 1967). Citroën had been taken over the previous year by Peugeot, and the pattern was repeated in 1981 when RVI took over the British and Spanish Dodge truck businesses which had been owned by Peugeot since their acquisition from Chrysler at the end of 1978. The Saviem and Berliet names were finally phased out in 1980. The year before, Renault acquired a 20% stake in Mack, the American truck manufacturer, and has exported trucks from France for sale as Macks in the USA. Since 1983, the former Dodge plant at Dunstable has assembled an increasing number of indigenous Renault trucks for sale on the British market. Overall, however, RVI is one of the heaviest loss-makers among Europe's truck manufacturers.

Saviem SM

Country of origin: France
Weight range: 32.5 to 38 tonnes
Engines: MAN
Cab/bonnet layout: Forward control

Saviem first entered the British market in 1974 with its SM32.240 32.5-tonne tractive unit powered by a 202hp MAN engine and fitted with the same Saviem cab as is fitted on MAN's F range trucks. It was joined two years later by the SM36.280 36-tonner and the SM38.280 38-tonner which were powered by a 242hp MAN turbocharged engine. They were discontinued after the Saviem and Berliet ranges were merged in 1978.

Above:
The similarity between the Saviem SM and the MAN F range is clear. This is an SM36 280.

Renault/Berliet TR/TF/R

Country of origin: France
Weight range: 34.5 to 40 tonnes
Engines: Berliet, Renault
Cab/bonnet layout: Forward control

Berliet's last heavy truck to be launched under Citroën control was the 38-tonne TR launched in 1972 and available in Britain from 1974. It has the same high, square KB2400

Below:
A Renault TR280 tractive unit, showing the open-slatted grille design which first appeared on Berliet-badged models.

cab which Berliet supplied to Ford for the Transcontinental, but is distinguished by a more open, horizontally-slatted grille with the headlamps and trafficators mounted on either side. Top model was the TR320 with a 320hp Berliet Maxi Couple V8 engine, but there was also a TR280 with a 240hp turbocharged six-cylinder engine and, from 1978, a TR305 40-tonner with a 298hp turbocharged and charge-cooled six-cylinder engine. It was followed by a 34.5-tonner, the TF231, with a 216hp engine. From 1980, the range was changed to the R range, and although the V8-engined model continued to be supplied to French customers, British operators were restricted to the R310 with a 307hp turbocharged and charge-cooled six-cylinder engine. Later models have a wider black grille with the headlamps mounted in the bumper.

Below:
A Berliet TR305 hauling a two-axle semi-trailer.

Renault/Saviem J range

Country of origin: France
Weight range: 7.5 to 13 tonnes
Engines: Renault, MAN
Cab/bonnet layout: Forward control

Saviem gave British operators their first chance of buying a product of the so-called 'Club of Four' partnership whereby Daf, Magirus, Saviem and Volvo joined forces to develop light to medium weight trucks with common components. The J range of JK, JN and JP 7.5- to 13-tonners first came to Britain in 1976 and remained on sale until 1982 when the Dodge takeover made it more prudent to satisfy the British market with the better selling Commando range. The cab is a symmetrical design, with the grille mirroring the windscreen in shape and with the rear of the cab door sloping forward slightly. The headlamps are incorporated into the grille.

Above:
A 13-tonne Saviem JP13 demountable van with Club of Four cab. Peter Rowlands

GF/TF/G

Country of origin: France, England
Weight range: 16 to 38 tonnes
Engines: Renault
Cab/bonnet layout: Forward control

Like the J range, the 1978 Renault G uses the Club of Four cab, but in larger form and with the headlamps moved to the bumper. First model on the British market was the 16-tonne GF151 which was on sale in 1980, and the TF231 was re-cabbed to this design. They were followed by a series of models assembled at Dunstable from 1983. The first

Below:
A Renault GF151, with enlarged Club of Four cab, heads through winter weather.

of these was the G260 38-tonne tractive unit or drawbar outfit with 258hp engine, then the G170 169hp 16-tonner replaced the GF151, and late-1985 saw the introduction of the G230 227hp 32.5-tonne tractive unit and the G290 287hp 38-tonner. Both of the 38-tonners are available in 6×2 form, thanks to conversion work by York Truck Engineering.

Below:
A heavy-duty Renault G170 16-tonner with sleeper cab and sliding-door box body.
Peter Rowlands

Bottom:
Top of the Club of Four range built in Britain by Renault is the G290 tractive unit for 38-tonne operation. It has a raised cab roof.

Reynolds-Boughton

The Amersham, Buckinghamshire-based Reynolds-Boughton business specialises in commercial vehicle body building, fire engine manufacture and four-wheel-drive conversion and vehicle manufacture.

RB44

Country of origin: England
Weight range: 5 tonnes
Engines: Ford, Bedford, Perkins, Rover
Cab/bonnet layout: Normal control

The four-wheel-drive RB44 was launched in 1978 and has been sold mainly for use by public utility undertakings. The axles and four-wheel-drive transfer box is built by Reynolds-Boughton, and although Bedford, Perkins and Rover engines have been offered, it is usually fitted with a Ford engine and gearbox. Until 1983, the company used Ford A-Series cabs, with its own vertically-slatted radiator grille in place of the subtler Ford grille, but later models have Dodge 50-Series cabs.

Below:
A Somerset Fire Brigade Reynolds-Boughton RB44 with Ford A-Series cab.

Roman

Interprinderea de Autocomione Brasov builds trucks in Romania under licence from West European manufacturers, notably MAN. Its Roman medium-weight range was sold in Britain between 1976 and 1981.

Country of origin: Romania
Weight range: 12.8 to 16 tonnes
Engines: Roman
Cab/bonnet layout: Forward control

The 12.8-tonne and 16-tonne Roman is a scaled down version of the F range MAN sold in Britain from 1974, having the same Saviem-designed cab, but a 135hp six-cylinder engine of MAN design. Both engine and cab were assembled in Romania.

Below:
A Roman 8.135F 12.8-tonner with Romanian-assembled MAN and Saviem components.

Saviem

See Renault

Scammell

Although it has been a Leyland subsidiary since 1955, Watford-based Scammell Lorries has preserved more of a separate identity than other companies absorbed into the Leyland empire. It owes much of that to its role as a special vehicle or low volume producer for its parent. In addition to trucks built with its own name, it manufactures eight-wheel Constructor and three-axle Roadtrain tractive units for Leyland. Until 1968 it built a range of three-wheeled urban delivery articulated vehicles (Scarab and Townsman) which found most favour with British Railways.

Highwayman

Country of origin: England
Weight range: Heavy haulage
Engines: Leyland, Gardner
Cab/bonnet layout: Normal control

Scammell launched its normal control Highwayman heavy haulage tractive unit in 1955 and kept it in production until 1970. They were available with Leyland or Gardner engines, had two-piece curved windscreens, exposed radiators and, on later models, twin headlamps.

Contractor

Country of origin: England
Weight range: Heavy haulage
Engines: Cummins, Rolls-Royce, AEC
Cab/bonnet layout: Normal control

For operation at up to 75 tonnes, Scammell developed its Contractor heavy haulage tractor in 1964 and offered it with a choice of AEC, Rolls-Royce and Cummins engines. Behind its mammoth bonnet, the standard cab was the Motor Panels LAD used on Leylands and Albions, but many Contractors were fitted with coachbuilt crew cabs to accommodate the large numbers of people often engaged in the heaviest movements of industrial equipment.

Left:
A Gardner 6LX-engined Scammell Highwayman normal control tractive unit with a low loading trailer from which the rear wheels have been removed for loading.
George Brown

Above:
A Scammell Contractor, with coachbuilt cab, pulling an abnormal load through outer London, while a similar vehicle pushes it from behind.

Routeman

Country of origin: England
Weight range: 30 tonnes
Engines: Leyland, Rolls-Royce
Cab/bonnet layout: Forward control

Scammell's two-year-old Routeman eight-wheeler was relaunched in 1962 with glass fibre cab designed, like the Leyland Ergomatic which would follow two years later, by Michelotti. The same cab was also fitted to the Handyman tractive unit built between 1964 and 1970, but it lasted until 1980 on the Routeman. It is distinguished by its almost egg-like shape, by the ribs around the middle and by the two-piece curved windscreen. It was offered with Leyland 680 or TL11 engines or a 220hp Rolls-Royce engine and was Britain's best-selling eight-wheeler until it was replaced by the Scammell-built Constructor in 1980.

Below:
A Scammell Routeman eight-wheeler with the stylish Michelotti-designed glass fibre cab which lasted in production for 18 years.

Crusader

Country of origin: England
Weight range: 32.5 to 44 tonnes
Engines: Rolls-Royce, Cummins, Detroit Diesel
Cab/bonnet layout: Forward control

The Crusader tractive unit was launched in 1968 as a 44-tonner with a 290hp Detroit Diesel 8V71 two-stroke engine, but sold mainly for heavy haulage work in that form as political pressures prevented an anticipated increase in maximum permitted lorry weights. The cab is a taller and wider version of the Motor Panels cab fitted on Guy and Seddon vehicles, but is disguised by a divided windscreen and a rectangular, upright radiator surround. It became much more common from September 1971, when the first 32.5-tonners developed for British Road Services were unveiled. BRS wanted a British truck to match the standards set by Scanias in its fleet, and specified the 220hp Rolls-Royce engine in the 4×2 Crusader. Some later examples were fitted with Cummins engines and others were built by Guy. Production ended in 1980, when the Leyland Roadtrain became available.

Top:
A heavy haulage Scammell Crusader 6×4 tractive unit in the Pickfords Industrial fleet.

Above:
A Rolls-Royce-engined Scammell Crusader 4×2 32.5-tonne tractive unit. The cab is a standard Motor Panels product.

S24

Country of origin: England
Weight range: Heavy haulage
Engines: Cummins
Cab/bonnet layout: Normal control

Scammell's 1980 S24 heavy haulage tractor for use at up to 200 tonnes is a bonneted design. It uses a 326hp Cummins 14-litre engine and the G-cab from the Bathgate-built home market vehicles and the Landtrain export truck also built at Watford. Like the Landtrain, it has a large meshed grille.

Above:
Behind the bonnet of the Scammell S24 is the G-cab used on Leyland's much lighter Bathgate-built trucks.

S26

Country of origin: England
Weight range: Heavy haulage
Engines: Cummins
Cab/bonnet layout: Forward control

The forward control S26 has the same engine and maximum operating weight of its bonneted cousin, the S24, but is fitted with the wide C40 cab from the Leyland Roadtrain. Cuprinol, the wood preservative company, has some in use as drawbar combinations.

Below:
An eight-wheel military version of Scammell's S26 forward control heavy haulage truck. Commercial Motor

Scania

Saab-Scania, based at Sodertalje, in Sweden, makes commercial vehicles, cars and aircraft. Scania has been in the commercial vehicle business since the early days of the century, and from 1911 until 1969, when it merged with Saab, was known as Scania-Vabis. It has been selling trucks in Britain since 1968, and its British operations are now centred on Milton Keynes.

LB range

Country of origin: Sweden, Belgium
Weight range: 16 to 38 tonnes
Engines: Scania
Cab/bonnet layout: Forward control

The LB range, launched early in 1968 and manufactured until 1980, is suitable for all weights from 16 tonnes upwards. The 8-litre-engined LB80, suitable for 16 to 32.5 tonnes, was fitted with a lower cab than the more powerful and heavier LB110 (11 litres) and LB140 (14-litre V8). Three-axle models were designated LBS, and the introduction of a revised engine range in 1974 led to the models being redesignated LB81, 111 and 141. The cab design is basically square with horizontally slatted grille and equal depth side windows.

Above:
A Scania LB81, with lower sleeper cab, in 32.5-tonne articulated application.
Peter Rowlands

Right:
A taller cab on a Scania LB111 tractive unit. There are two more horizontal slats on the grille.

GPR range

Country of origin: Sweden, Belgium
Weight range: 16 to 38 tonnes
Engines: Scania
Cab/bonnet layout: Forward control

The GPR range, introduced in 1980 and available in Britain from 1981, has an entirely new cab with a raked windscreen, cab door windows without a quarterlight, and an overhanging section behind the front axle. It takes its name from the three optional cab designs. G is a low profile cab for urban distribution, P is the basic cab for general haulage, and R is the top specification cab for long distance work.

British operators have the choice of the G82 16.5-tonner and P82 16.5- to 34.5-tonner with 7.8-litre engine, the G92 16-tonner and P92 16.6- to 38-tonner with 8.5-litre engine, the P112 or R112 tractive unit with 11-litre engine, or the R142 tractive unit with 14.2-litre engine. Suffix letters shown on the front beside the model number denote whether the vehicle is for medium duty (M), heavy duty (H) or extra heavy duty (E).

T142E

Country of origin: Sweden
Weight range: Heavy haulage
Engines: Scania
Cab/bonnet layout: Normal control

The bonneted Scania T range was launched in 1980, before the GPR range, and uses the same cab designs. Only one model, the T142E, is sold in Britain — as a heavy haulage tractor for work at up to 178 tonnes gross.

Left:
One of Britain's newer overnight parcels delivery companies, ANC of Stoke-on-Trent, is the operator of this Scania P112M tractive unit.

Below left:
A Scania R112M 6×2 tractive unit hauls a sheeted load out of Dover.

Above:
A Scania T142E heavy haulage tractor operated in Sweden.

Seddon Atkinson

Seddon started building Perkins diesel-engined trucks in Salford in 1938, moved into former aircraft carburettor works in Oldham in 1948, and in 1970 took over the Atkinson business. In turn, the combined business was acquired four years later by International Harvester (IH), the American conglomerate which retained control until 1984, by which time poor trading by the parent group had prompted it to trim its sails. IH had also bought a stake in Enasa, the Spanish state-owned truck group, with a view to setting up an engine plant in Spain, and in the course of disposing of those shares also sold Seddon Atkinson to Enasa. By then, the former Atkinson factory at Walton-le-Dale had been closed and all manufacturing concentrated on the Oldham headquarters. Future development of vehicles is likely to be dominated by the Cabtech project to build a new range of cabs for Daf and Enasa lorries.

Seddon 14- to 32.5-tonner

Country of origin: England
Weight range: 14 to 32.5 tonnes
Engines: Perkins, Gardner, Rolls-Royce
Cab/bonnet layout: Forward control

The last range of Seddon, as opposed to Seddon Atkinson, trucks first appeared in 1965 when the company stopped using a glass fibre cab and instead fitted a Motor Panels cab similar to that on the Guy Big J. The large, horizontally-slatted grille with Seddon Diesel badge tells it apart. For operation at up to 28 tonnes, Perkins engines were standard; Gardner and Rolls-Royce engines were fitted in the heaviest vehicles. This model remained available for municipal work until the Seddon Atkinson 201 was launched in 1982.

200/300/400

Country of origin: England
Weight range: 14 to 32.5 tonnes
Engines: International Harvester, Gardner, Rolls-Royce, Cummins
Cab/bonnet layout: Forward control

A new design of Motor Panels cab was developed for the first generation of Seddon Atkinson trucks which first appeared in 1975. They have a slightly raked, curved windscreen, a cab door window with a shallow, divided opening section at the top, and a narrow window (two on a sleeper cab) behind the cab door. The 200 14-16-tonne rigid has a shallow grille with four horizontal slats, set at the bottom of the cab, while the 300 24-tonner and the 400 eight-wheel rigid and tractive unit have a deeper grille with five horizontal slats. The 400, fitted with Gardner, Rolls-Royce and Cummins engines, was developed from the Atkinson range and was available from 1975 to 1981. The 200, fitted with IH's DH358 134hp engine, was developed from the previous Seddon range and was available from 1976 to 1982. The 300, which started life with more IH technology including its DT466 196hp engine, was available from 1978 to 1982. A Seddon Atkinson badge, with the name in a logo of interlocking circles based on the rings used around the Seddon Diesel badge and the encircled 'A' of the Atkinson range, appears at the top right-hand corner of the grilles on the 300 and 400, and just above the top right-hand corner of the grille on the 200, but many customers of all three models fitted the Atkinson 'A' badge as an extra.

Above left:
A 1974 example of Seddon's 13- to 16-tonne tanker-bodied lorry with Perkins engine and Motor Panels cab. Alan Millar

Left:
A taller version of the Motor Panels cab and Seddon grille was fitted to the 32.5-tonne Seddon tractive unit.

Above:
A Seddon Atkinson 200 fitted with a demountable body. Peter Rowlands

Above:
A Seddon Atkinson 300 six-wheel tipper. Commercial Motor

Below:
A Seddon Atkinson 400 tractive unit with day cab. George Brown

201/301/401

Country of origin: England
Weight range: 14 to 38 tonnes
Engines: Perkins, International Harvester, Cummins, Gardner, Rolls-Royce
Cab/bonnet layout: Forward control

The updated Seddon Atkinson range shares the same basic cab design of the 200/300/400 range, but is distinguishable by a large rectangular grille with diagonal slats, a chrome effect surround, large Seddon Atkinson name at the top and the Atkinson 'A' in the centre. The 201, launched in 1982, has Perkins or IH engines; the 301, launched in 1982 and available as a six- or eight-wheel rigid or a lightweight tractive unit, has a Cummins L10 engine; and the 401 is offered with Gardner, Rolls-Royce or Cummins engines, and has been available since 1981.

Above:
A Seddon Atkinson 201 refuse collection vehicle operated at Heathrow Airport, London.

Below:
The Cummins L10-engined Seddon Atkinson 301 eight-wheel tipper.

Bottom:
A twin-steer Seddon Atkinson 401 6×2 tractive unit fitted with a sleeper cab.

2-11

Country of origin: England
Weight range: 16 to 24 tonnes (20/24 tonnes for Britannia only)
Engines: Perkins
Cab/bonnet layout: Forward control

The 201 16-tonner was replaced in July 1986 by the 2-11, a higher-powered model with lighter components to enable it to carry a greater payload. Standard engine is Perkins' new Phaser diesel, either the 173hp turbocharged and charge-cooled 180Ti for long

Below:
A Seddon Atkinson 2-11 with the full air deflection kit fitted.

Bottom:
A three-axle version of the Britannia municipal vehicle, based on the Seddon Atkinson 2-11 and fitted with an Alexander grp cab. It has a Britannia badge on the nearside, beneath the windscreen.

distance work or the 153hp turbocharged 160T for short haul work. Ogle Design restyled the Motor Panels cab to give it air deflectors ahead of the cab doors and at the back of the cab, as well as optional under-bumper and roof spoilers. It has rectangular headlamps.

The 2-11 is also the basis for the Britannia Trucks range of municipal vehicles built for Jack Allen of Birmingham. It uses a glass-reinforced plastic yellow cab made by Alexander, the Scottish bus and train builder, and fitted to the chassis at Oldham. It is a square cab, with one-piece windscreen, cab door and crew cab window sloping up to the rear, and a bus-type two-piece inward folding nearside door to help dustcart crews get on and off quickly. 20- and 24-tonne three-axle versions are also built. Standard cab is 2.5m wide, but a 2.2m narrow version is also made.

Shelvoke

Shelvoke and Drewry started building commercial vehicles at Letchworth, Hertfordshire, primarily for the municipal market in 1922, and became a subsidiary of the Butterfield-Harvey engineering group 44 years later. Its commanding share of the British market for refuse collection vehicles has been lost in recent years to Dennis and to the larger truck manufacturers, but it survives in partnership with Dempster, the American dustcart specialist, and since 1984 has traded as Shelvoke Dempster. It developed a business in selling special-purpose vehicles to customers' individual designs in the 1970s.

T-type

Country of origin: England
Weight range: 8 to 16 tonnes
Engines: Perkins, Leyland, Bedford
Cab/bonnet layout: Forward control

Production of the T-type ran from 1959 to 1977, with 11,000 being sold. It has a glass fibre cab with two-piece curved windscreen, vertically-divided grille with 'SD' logo and cab door windows without quarterlights. Perkins, Bedford and Leyland engines were fitted.

A Shelvoke and Drewry T-type refuse collection vehicle, with its prominent 'SD' logo in the grille. The narrow TN remained in production until 1977. George Brown

N-type

Country of origin: England
Weight range: 11.5 to 22.4 tonnes
Engines: Leyland, Perkins, Ford, Mercedes-Benz
Cab/bonnet layout: Forward control

Shelvoke turned to Motor Panels for the cab for its N-type built between 1972 and 1979. The design is based on the cab used by Guy and Seddon on general haulage vehicles, but has a cab extension to give crews additional headroom. Around 3,000 were built.

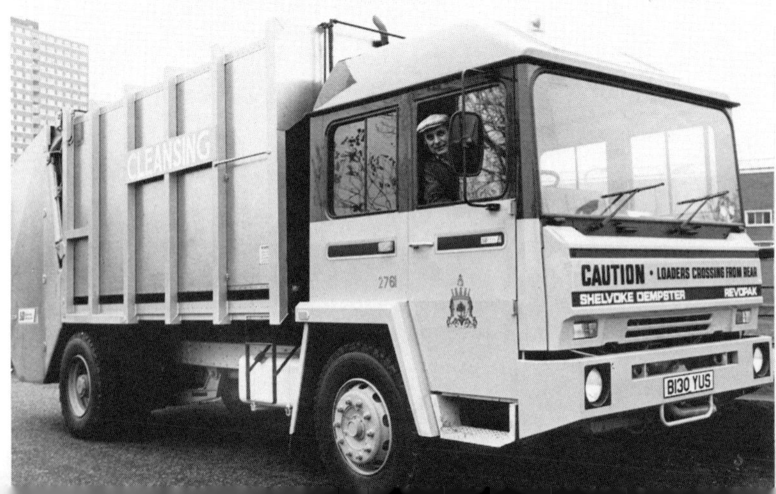

Below left:
The steel cabbed Shelvoke and Drewry N-type, with Motor Panels cab heightened and lengthened to accommodate a standing crew, was built from 1972 to 1979.

Bottom left:
A Shelvoke Dempster P-type, with Revopak body, in the yellow and green Glasgow District Council livery. Glasgow is one of the biggest Shelvoke operators.

P-type

Country of origin: England
Weight range: 8 to 22.4 tonnes
Engines: Leyland, Perkins, Rolls-Royce
Cab/bonnet layout: Forward control

Ogle Design, the Letchworth company also responsible for the Dennis cab for the 1980s, developed a similarly-shaped tilt cab for the P-series of dustcarts offered from 1978. Similar cabs were fitted on fire engines and other special-purpose vehicles built by Shelvoke.

Stonefield

Stonefield Vehicles was established by Jim McKelvie, the former Scottish road haulier who set up Volvo's British truck and bus import organisation, as a manufacturer of all-terrain off-road vehicles. Production began in 1977 at Cumnock, Ayrshire with support from the Scottish Development Agency. McKelvie's early death deprived the business of some of its momentum and it went into receivership in 1980. It was taken over by Abdul Shamji's Gomba trading group the following year and renamed Gomba Stonefield. Production moved to Rochester, Kent in 1983.

Country of origin: Scotland, England
Weight range: Built for special applications
Engines: Chrysler, Ford
Cab/bonnet layout: Forward control

The limited number of Stonefields built — most of them by the original owner — are identifiable as box-like forward-control vehicles with a raked windscreen. They have Chrysler or Ford petrol engines and automatic gearboxes. Gomba intended to sell the vehicles, which had military potential, with Perkins diesel engines and manual gearboxes.

Right:
A Stonefield 6×4 on/off-highway truck used for drilling work. George Brown

Volvo

Volvo has been building trucks since 1928, and has been selling them in Britain since 1967. Most are built in Sweden, but it also has a plant at Ghent in Belgium, and another at Irvine in Ayrshire which modifies vehicles for the British market and makes special low volume models for the Swiss and Swedish markets.

F86

Country of origin: Sweden, Scotland
Weight range: 24 to 32.5 tonnes
Engines: Volvo
Cab/bonnet layout: Forward control

The F86 was Volvo's first truck on the British market and remained available until 1978. It was built for 24- to 32.5-tonne work as a three- or four-axle rigid or as a tractive unit, and has Volvo's own TD70 turbocharged 6.7-litre engine. The cab is raked at the front, has a large rectangular grille occupying most of the bottom half of the cab front and incorporating the headlamps, and has a round-topped cab door with the quarterlights set at a lower level in line with the bottom of the windscreen.

Below:
A six-wheel Volvo F86 fitted with a platform body. George Brown

F88/F89

Country of origin: Sweden
Weight range: 32.5 tonnes
Engines: Volvo
Cab/bonnet layout: Forward control

The F88 and F89, heavier and more powerful models than the F86, went into production in 1965 and first came to Britain in 1968. The cab bears a resemblance to that of the F86, but is higher, has the cab door entirely above the front axle, a divided windscreen, and the grille set higher up the cab and above the headlights. They remained available until 1977.

Above:
A Volvo F88 tractive unit hard at work hauling deep sea containers. Commercial Motor

F6/F7

Country of origin: Sweden, Belgium, Scotland
Weight range: 16 to 38 tonnes
Engines: Volvo
Cab/bonnet layout: Forward control

The F6 and F7 share the Club of Four cab also used in Britain on Renault G-range trucks and fitted in Europe to Daf and Magirus models. The F6, available in Britain from 1980 and built in Belgium, is a 16-tonner fitted with a 5.5-litre Volvo TD60 engine, while the F7, available since 1978 as a replacement for the F86, has the TD70 engine. They were replaced by new FL-range trucks in 1985.

Below:
A Volvo F616, the 16-tonne version of the F6 sold in Britain.

Above:
A British-built Volvo F7 eight-wheeler used for waste disposal.

Below:
A sleeper-cabbed Volvo F7 tractive unit and bulk tanker semi-trailer.

F10/F12

Country of origin: Sweden, Scotland
Weight range: 32.5 to 59.5 tonnes
Engines: Volvo
Cab/bonnet layout: Forward control

The F10, powered by the 10-litre TD100 diesel, and the 12-litre TD120-powered F12 replaced the F88 and F89 in 1977. They have a squarer cab design with a large rectangular grille occupying most of the front area beneath the windscreen. Later models have a larger windscreen.

Below:
A Volvo F10 with tri-axle tipping semi-trailer.

Bottom:
A top-of-the-range Volvo F12 tractive unit and two-axle van-bodied trailer.

FL4/FL6

Country of origin: Belgium
Weight range: 7.5 to 16 tonnes
Engines: Volvo
Cab/bonnet layout: Forward control

The Volvo range was extended further in Britain when the 12- to 16-tonne FL6 was launched in 1985. Its cab is lower than that on the F6, but the profile and some mouldings are carried over. The most distinguishing feature is the very deep cab door glazing — in fact a slightly deeper quarterlight and a lower kerbside viewing window in a matt black moulding — to help drivers when manoeuvring in tight spaces. It uses Volvo's TD61 engine.

An even smaller Volvo, the FL4 7.5-tonner with 3.6-litre engine, was launched at the 1986 Amsterdam Motor Show and becomes available in Britain early in 1987. It uses the same cab as the FL6, but has much smaller wheels.

Above:
An 11-tonne Volvo FL6 chassis/cab, showing the deep cab door viewing window disguised as a very deep quarterlight.

Below:
The Volvo FL4 is exactly as it looks, a scaled-down version of the FL6.

FL7/FL10

Country of origin: Sweden, Belgium, Scotland
Weight range: 16 to 38 tonnes
Engines: Volvo
Cab/bonnet layout: Forward control

The 1985 low-cab replacements for the F7 bear a strong resemblance to Scania's GPR range, most notably the raked windscreen, square cab profile and overhanging rear

Above:
There is a hint of Scania in the styling of Volvo's FL7, in this case a tractive unit used for coal haulage by an Oxfordshire operator. The opening area of the cab door windows is within the line running to the left of and above the nearside wing mirror.
Peter Rowlands

Below:
A Volvo N10 heavy-haulage tractor hauling a crane section into Felixstowe docks.

section. Unlike the Scania, the Volvo's cab door window is deeper at the front, where a quarterlight might have been provided. Only about half of the cab door window area opens. The FL7 has the TD71 engine, while the FL10 has the TD100 engine to match the F10's power to a lower and less sophisticated cab specification.

N10/N12

Country of origin: Sweden
Weight range: Heavy haulage
Engines: Volvo
Cab/bonnet layout: Normal control

The normal control N10 and N12 have been available since 1974 and have sold in small numbers in Britain, notably for heavy off-road work or for heavy haulage. They use the TD100 and TD120 engines from the F10 and F12, have raked windscreens and round-topped side windows.

White

The White Truck Corporation, based at Dublin, Virginia, in the United States, has been building internal combustion-engined trucks since 1909. It expanded in postwar years by acquiring smaller American truck builders, but in 1981 was rescued from the jaws of obscurity by Volvo, which changed its name to Volvo White. Now, it builds European-designed trucks in addition to the indigenous American range and has taken some of Volvo's British management in the process. It sold trucks in Britain briefly before the Volvo takeover.

Road Commander 2

Country of origin: United States
Weight range: 32.5 to 38 tonnes
Engines: Caterpillar
Cab/bonnet layout: Forward control

A British agent, White Truck Concessionaires, imported the Road Commander 2 tractive unit to Britain from 1978. It is powered by an American engine, the Caterpillar 3406 325hp diesel. The cab is unmistakably American, being tall with a divided windscreen, large square grille divided vertically, and with the front axle set forward.

Below:
A White Road Commander 2 operated on international refrigerated transport from Britain to Europe. Commercial Motor